Robert Harborough Sherard

The White Slaves of England

Being True Pictures of Certain Social Conditions in the Kingdom of England in the

Year 1897

Robert Harborough Sherard

The White Slaves of England
Being True Pictures of Certain Social Conditions in the Kingdom of England in the Year 1897

ISBN/EAN: 9783744723671

Printed in Europe, USA, Canada, Australia, Japan

Cover: Foto ©ninafisch / pixelio.de

More available books at **www.hansebooks.com**

THE WHITE SLAVES OF ENGLAND

BEING TRUE PICTURES OF CERTAIN SOCIAL
CONDITIONS IN THE KINGDOM
OF ENGLAND IN THE
YEAR 1897

BY
ROBERT HARBOROUGH SHERARD

AUTHOR OF "JACOB NIEMAND" "THE
MOCKING-BIRD" ETC

ILLUSTRATED BY
HAROLD PIFFARD

"Zwischen dem Ambos
und Hammer"
—*Goethe*

LONDON: JAMES BOWDEN
10 HENRIETTA STREET
COVENT GARDEN WC
1897

Un long cri d'indignation retentit en ce moment en Europe à la suite des révélations faites par M. Sherard.

L'Intransigeant (Paris)
January 4, 1897

TRANSLATION

A long cry of indignation is echoing to-day through Europe, in consequence of the revelations made by Mr. Sherard.

L'Intransigeant (Paris)

To My Friend,
THE REV. HERBERT BENTLEY FREEMAN,
SENIOR CURATE OF ST. ANNE'S, SOHO,
This Book is Dedicated.

Contents

	PAGE
PREFACE	15
ORIGINAL PREFACE	41
THE ALKALI WORKERS	47
THE NAILMAKERS	81
THE SLIPPER-MAKERS AND TAILORS	111
THE WOOLCOMBERS	141
THE WHITE-LEAD WORKERS	173
THE CHAINMAKERS	207
APPENDIX	241

List of Illustrations

	PAGE
Done to Death . . . . . . *Frontispiece*	
Costume of a Bleaching-powder Packer	55
Slain by " Roger "	57
"The Factories, though spacious, are Mean and Dirty"	59
A Stone Nobbler (8*d.* the ton)	63
Drawing the Black Ash from a Revolving Furnace .	67
" These men literally carry their lives in their hands "	71
" Numerous are the stories of men boiled to death in the steaming Caustic-pots ".	73
Some of the Bromsgrove Nailmakers	82
The Nailmakers' Cottages	85
No Iron	87
Interior of a Bromsgrove Nailmaker's Shed . .	89
"Seven shillings a week "	95
Delivering the Nails at the Factory	99
" He had worked at the trade for seventy-seven years "	105
A slipper-maker's home—Past ten at night . .	115
In a Jew slipper factory	119
Fitting toe-caps to slipper-tops	123
" When one of these endless band-knives does break, you never know where it's going to fly to " .	127
" The gaunt Sweater stalks about scolding " . .	129
" The Foreman kept us waiting a day and a half " .	135
Tired out	137

14 LIST OF ILLUSTRATIONS

	PAGE
Bradford Woolcombers going home from work in the early morning	113
In the Woolcombers' Club	116
The Walking Skeleton	151
"Not twelve shillings a week all the years I've worked"	153
In the Carding Room	163
"A smoke of 'bacca in the Wash-house"	169
White-Bed Women with their "Muzzles" on	175
Blue-Bed Women with Trucks of Lead	185
A Tan Carrier	189
A Corner of a White-lead Factory	193
A Sifter	197
A Red-lead Furnace Man	201
A Group of Cradley Heath Chainmakers	209
"It appeared that she had influential relations"	213
"A woman plying her task in a cell-like shed"	221
"Her work lasted twelve hours a day"	230
"A particular and pitiful sight"	231
Apprenticed to the Art and Trade of Chainmaking	234
Three Farthings Apiece	237

Preface

IT is my duty—a pleasant duty—in republishing these articles descriptive of the horrible slavery to which so many thousands of our country men and women are subjected, to express in the foremost place my obligation to Mr. C. Arthur Pearson, in whose magazine these life-stories appeared last year.

It was thanks to his enterprise and unstinted liberality that I was able to carry out my investigations as fully as the gravity of the subject demanded; it was thanks to his courage that a first hearing by millions of people all over the world was obtained for the very serious charges which in these papers are brought against the English industrial system.

In writing of "millions of people all over the world," I do not over-rate. *Pearson's Magazine* goes to the four corners of the earth, and on one and the same day I received a Japanese newspaper from Japan and an English newspaper from Jamaica containing long extracts from these articles. They have been quoted in every country of Europe, and in every State in America; they have formed the subject of sermons from the pulpit and of lectures from the platform.

In saying this, let me not be suspected of self-complacency nor accused of self-flattery. I have but little share in the triumph of arousing this universal interest. These are life-stories told in their own language by unhappy men and women. I was but the scrivener who took these stories down, and thus any one of Mr. Pearson's printers who helped in putting them into type deserves as much credit as myself.

To Mr. Pearson, on the other hand, all credit is due. Sympathetic from the first to our poor friends, he boldly faced the odium which might have been aroused against him in the " classes " by lending his magazine to the purposes of these arraignments. His was the risk, his was the courage, and his should be the honour.

PREFACE

For my part, I attribute this universal interest to the universal desire for knowledge of the truth about contemporary social conditions. The great success which has attended on M. Zola or Mr. Arthur Morrison, as novelists, and on Mr. Robert Blatchford, amongst others, as chroniclers, is due, without any doubt, to the fact that all these writers, realists of fiction or of fact, are known to speak the truth. And I believe that all those who told me their dismal stories, as set forth in these pages, men, women, and children, did also speak the truth. "We ums no interest to tell you no lies" was said to me over and over again by haggard witnesses, in the course of my long cross-examinations. Nor had they. I have been told by employers since these articles have been published that the men have been "kidding me" or "getting at me," resenting the interference of a stranger in their affairs. I am very sure that this is not so. One has eyes to see as well as ears to hear, and no secondary evidence was put into the world which direct evidence had not confirmed. And as to being "kidded," I do not think I lack in experience. I wanted the truth, for the truth alone was of value to me; the lie must defeat itself. Indeed, to the credit of all the workers whom I examined, I will say that I only remember one instance where deliberate "getting at" was attempted. This was done by a chainmaker at Cradley Heath, with whom I wasted the best part of a day, and who, indeed, "kidded" me merrily. He told me that the highest wages a male chainmaker could earn were 20*s.* a week, and so on. But his lies were anæmic and short-lived. I turned his depositions into pipe-spills, and consigned his words to temporary oblivion.

It has also been advanced that as in each case I put myself under the guidance of the secretary of the local trades union, and was by him introduced to the persons who told me their pitiful stories, my witnesses were naturally the most miserable members of each trade, non-representative, in a word, so that I have only shown the worst side of the question. This is not so. The various secretaries, to whose kindness I owe so much, all expressed the hope and wish that I should write in a fair and impartial spirit, for they knew, as I knew, that untruth or exaggeration would but injure the cause which we had so much at heart. In each case, I noticed a wish that justice should be done, and, indeed, where any extenuating circumstance could be adduced, it was put forward with extreme alacrity. I remember with what satisfaction Mr. Samuel Shaftoe, J.P., Secretary of the Woolcombers' Association, informed me, in answer to my question whether to his knowledge any of the miserably underpaid slaves of Bradford had been able to put by any money out of their scanty and irregular wages as a provision against sickness, or for old age, that he knew of a couple—man and wife—who had saved up the sum of £60. And he rubbed his hands and I rubbed mine.

Moreover, it was not to the secretaries of unions nor to union men alone that I addressed myself. Indeed, I saw more non-Unionists, and this for the simple reason that in these particular trades it is but the minority which dares thus syndicate itself.

These are trades in which capital is allpowerful, tyrannical, indeed, in which the supply of flesh and bone largely exceeds the demand; in which haggard men and women and children fight for the privilege of joining in a sordid dance of death, so that but the few dare assert any other rights than to feed and work and rot and die, lest the masters take offence, and the crust be withheld. For the crust is sweet, albeit poison-laden, and these people cling to dear life with a tenacity which is the philosopher's admiration. It was Dostoïevski, was it not, who said that the instinct for living is so great in the human race that a man would prefer life to death even though this life had to be passed standing on a rock in mid-ocean, the head alone above the water. And, in despite of pain and sickness and the terrible fardel of moral degradation which these helots have to bear, in despite of the chilling hopelessness of the immediate future, in despite of the certainty of an ugly and premature death, life is dearer to these poor men and women than ever it is to the scented coxcombs of our promenades. And so it is that but the few dare to do anything that may bring a frown on to the master's narrow brow, that may jeopardize the insufficient loaf, that may starve, indeed, those who have only been hungry all their lives.

"None of Healey's men need apply" was an edict recently given forth in Widnes and St. Helens. Patrick Healey is the secretary of the Chemical Workers' Union in these two towns, the adherents to which, as stated, were boycotted on this occasion, as on many others.[1] It is the same everywhere, and the result, as I have said, is that it is but the few who dare to combine for the protection of their rights. Rights! poor fellows!

So I saw non-Union men as well as Union men. It was the same story with those as with these.

In the prefatory note which preceded the articles in *Pearson's Magazine,* and which is

---

[1] Since writing these lines I have heard that, as a result of this boycotting, The Chemical Workers' Union has been broken up, the club houses at St. Helens and Widnes have been closed, and the furniture in these sold by auction. Thus the last little defence that these poor fellows had against their masters has been destroyed. God help them.

printed in this book also, I describe the manner in which I worked. A few further particulars may be of interest. Before giving these, however, I have a further disclaimer to make. I know very well—as well as those who have pointed the circumstance out to me—that in this matter of the White Slaves of England I am no discoverer; that all these things have been described before again and again, notably in a splendid series of articles which appeared in 1892 in the *Daily Chronicle*, entitled "Danger in the Workshop," and that even the title has been used over and over again. I knew this when I undertook the work. I know it now. But these are matters where silence is felony, of which the evil must be ever and ever shouted from the house-tops till not a man or woman in the British Isles can plead ignorance as an excuse for indifference of the abominations in our midst which should make one ashamed of the name of Englishman.[1] Till now, little,

---

[1] Writes David Christie Murray, in the preface to his striking novel, "A Capful o' Nails," which deals with the Nailmakers: "Much is amended now-a-days,

if anything, has been done for all the masterly exposures of these iniquities. Parliamentary Commissions have been held, a special enquiry has been made on behalf of the Home Office, and the state of these people is worse than ever it was. I can think only of one particular reform which is to result from these Commissions, and that is that after June of this year it will be illegal to employ women in the white lead factories. This is an excellent reform, as all those will agree who read in the pages devoted to the white lead industry of the martyrdom of Elizabeth Ryan, aged nineteen, and late of 23, Silver Street, Newcastle-on-Tyne, a single example of many martyrdoms.[1] But that is all, whilst, *per contra*, in the matter of wages and imposition of tasks, everywhere things are growing worse and worse. Should women be allowed to

but the truth even to-day is stern and mournful, and may well make an Englishman ashamed."

[1] A few weeks after I had left Newcastle-on-Tyne, Mr. Innes, of the *Newcastle Leader*, kindly sent me the report of an inquest held on another young woman, who had died under circumstances identical with those of the death of poor Elizabeth.

do blacksmiths' work, and at a starvation wage? Imagine a woman, within a few hours, nay, minutes, of becoming a mother, working the treadle of the heavy hammer, impeded by the disfigurement of her approaching maternity, yet fighting against all physical disabilities for a few more farthings.[1] So whilst these things continue to be, so long must the cry of reprobation be raised, till every corner in the land echoes with the shout of "Shame!"

As I explain in the prefatory note which follows this preface, I did not, on a single occasion, apply to any master for permission to enter the jealously-guarded workshops. I thought it would be an act of *lèse*-hospitality to accept a favour and afterwards to criticise and attack, if occasion arose, as I anticipated it would arise. My entire time was spent with the workpeople, of whom I can say that people more hospitable and kindly I have never met. They had little or no interest in my work; experience has made fatalists

---

[1] I say farthings deliberately. The wages of these blacksmith women must be calculated not by pence, but by farthings per hour.

of them all; they have forgotten how to hope; of all these stirs and alarms nothing has ever come, and they expect nothing but the "grubber," struggling on with a resignation and courage which are little less than sublime. As an alleged would-be exposer of their wrongs, I was to them but another sleek humbug in a frock coat and a tall hat, with private ends to gain, for whom they cared nothing, of whom they wanted nothing; but as a man who evidently sympathized with them, and respected them, as I did respect them, whose work is so much finer because so much more manly, so much more courageous than this unmanly trade of writing, they took me to their loyal hearts, and held out their grimy hands and passed the mug of beer.

An instance of their hospitality. In one town I found myself one night likely to be homeless. It was a small town, and the only possible hotel there closed at eleven o'clock, after which hour admittance was given to none. I had arrived late in the afternoon—it was my second visit—and had gone straight to the workmen's club, where

I had spent the whole evening in conversation with the members. Our meeting broke up at midnight, and I made my way at once to the hotel, accompanied by a couple of the workmen, who had warned me that I should ring at the door in vain. And so it was, so that at half-past twelve I found myself in the street, a homeless man. Here was a good opportunity, I thought, to see this town by night, or rather, I should say, to smell it by night; for the fact had been vouchsafed to me that the factories there used to let off their foul and noxious gases in the early hours of the morning, when all the folk were asleep, thus evading certain pains and penalties edicted by Government for contravening stringent regulations. The prospect of such a *nuit blanche* was not a pleasing one, even to one accustomed to late-walking, and in quest of experiences; but as I wanted to see, hear, and even smell all things for myself, I should have faced it, had the weather not suddenly changed and come on to rain heavily. Then I saw the two workmen in whispered confabulation. At last one approached me and said : " Gaffer, thou canst not stay out the night. Thou shalt come home with me." I remonstrated, but in the end accepted his hospitality. We walked a long way, but his cottage was at last reached, a four-roomed hovel, for which he paid five shillings a week, work and wages or no work and no wages. He left me in the kitchen, with a "Bide a bit, gaffer," and darted upstairs. Presently I heard him cry, "Get up lass, and out of that. There's a gentleman going to sleep here to-night." It suddenly dawned upon me that there was but one bed in this poor house, and that my host was turning his wife out of it, to make room for his guest. I called him down and told him that on no consideration was he to disturb Madame, and when he insisted, I prepared to leave the house. At last he gave in, and I made myself comfortable on three chairs. In the morning, when I awoke, I found breakfast on the table, round which my host and hostess and four bonny children were sitting. We had bread without butter and tea without milk. I remained in that cottage the best part of the day, and talked the whole time with the woman of the house, the children and the neighbours, who, in spite of explanations, persisted in taking me for the man in possession. It was a day of poignant interest, in the insight it gave me into all the mean miseries of the very poor. I heard about the landlord's tyrannies, the rapacity of the credit-giving and usurious tradesmen, of the terrible difficulties which the good lady of the house had to face, with six mouths to feed out of scanty and irregular wages.

I could mention many similar instances of kindly hospitality; indeed, I may say that there was but one occasion, and one occasion only, on which I was treated with rudeness, and this was at Bradford, where a drunken woolcomber would have it that I was "a —— bum-bailiff," and offered personal violence. He was promptly challenged to fight by every other man in the pot-house, and it might have gone ill with him, had not the barman helped him out into the street.

I must say that I liked my life amongst these people, for all that every waking hour was fraught with some fresh experience of suffering. They are such good people, or, I should say, they are people with such excellent dispositions to be good, if only circumstances would let them be. They are cheerful—they to whom everything that gladdens life is wanting. They will laugh heartily—or it may be only hysterically—over the humorous aspects of their condition, for there is always something grotesque in extreme wretchedness. I shall not forget how the men at the Chemical Workers' Club in Widnes roared at the joke about the donkey, asphyxiated by Roger, or chlorine gas, who died manfully; and the one about a chemical worker having to pay a man five shillings to masticate his food for him. This last joke tickled them specially, and they grinned with their black gums. For hardly a man amongst them had saved his teeth from destruction—one of the perquisites of work in the chemical yards. I cannot say how I envied them their characters, how I admired them, how I respected them. The Girondins singing on their way to the scaffold showed not more heroism than these people do every day of their lives. A week spent in their company should cure the most confirmed pessimist. When men and women can keep up heart under conditions so terrible, who has a right to despair? Who has a right to vilify human nature, which in these people manifests itself so admirable, so heroic? I would like to take Dr. Ibsen and a few of his acolytes into some of the cottages and the workshops which I visited. It would give them a better opinion of humanity.

I think that I can give the record case of cheerfulness under adversity. In one workhouse I was introduced to an old workman named Peter. He was in bed, and looked very ill. But he laughed and rubbed his hands when asked how he was, and said, "It's coming off next week. Then I'll be all right." My companion, one of the guardians, said, "That's right, Peter." As we walked away he said to me: "The poor fellow was speaking of his leg. He was a worker in ——'s factory, and got blood-poisoning. One leg was amputated about six weeks ago. The remaining one is now quite gone; it's like black marble. The man is booked; he could not stand another operation, but to comfort him the doctors tell him that they will amputate it. You saw how pleased he was." The prospect of some diminution of his sufferings made this man laugh and rub his hands. When I reached the end of the ward, I turned round to take a last look at the poor old fellow, whose philosophy seemed to me so much finer, so much more laudable than all the thankless railings of Schopenhauer, Hartmann, Nietzsche, Ibsen, and the rest. And speaking of Ibsen reminds me of a remark I made to a woman in Cradley Heath, who was forging chain-harrows at three-farthings an hour: "I wish I could have put Hedda Gabler in your place for a month or two. It would have taken the nonsense out of her." This woman had six children and a drunken husband to keep, and worked fourteen hours a day for a weekly wage of six shillings. After two months of this work and this life, Fru Gabler would have returned to Christiania to laugh at her petty troubles, and we should never have had to hear the pistol-shot which throws the foolish into such contemptible ecstasies of emotion.

No doubt in these poor people the animal—

what Zola calls *la bête humaine*—is predominant, but for that who is to blame? Not they themselves in truth. There is no pleasure in their lives, as in the following pages is so often set forth in their own words; they have no time for relaxation; when in work and when out of work—playing!—their entire energy is taken up in the hunting of the loaf. Living lives far worse than the lives of domestic animals, how can it be a matter for wonder that in them the animal prevails? " We ums making childer whilst we's making chains," said a chain-woman to me, who added that her husband's embraces were the only joys that reconciled her to life. And then there's the drink. Smug correspondents have pointed out to me that by my own statement I interviewed most of the people, whose words are quoted in these articles, in public-houses, that people who frequent public-houses are naturally in difficulties, and do not merit any sympathy. Where else was I to see them? At my hotel? The innkeeper would have refused admittance to such draggled tatterdemalions. In their own houses? Well, where it was possible I did so visit them, but often it was inconvenient for them—for various reasons which I could easily guess—to receive me there. In one of the fashionable clubs in the town perhaps? *Va-t'en voir s'ils viennent, Jean.* I had the choice between the public-house and the street, and preferred the former.

As to the drinking of these people, I admit that they aggravate their position by this indulgence. But you cannot degrade a man beneath the level of brute beasts, as these men and women are degraded, and then expect of them restraint or self-respect. And further, it should be remembered that all these classes of work are so exhausting, so thirst-provoking, that the men must drink. Well, let them drink barley-water, or oatmeal-water, say you. A man who, by the nature of his work, is unable to eat anything, or to retain anything,[1] must keep his energies alive with stimulants. It is deplorable, it is fatal, but it is so. Let Chadband, instead of deploring effect—drunkenness—rather join us in deploring causes—degradation and

[1] See the doctor's remarks in the article on "The Chemical Workers."

unnatural conditions of life. Let the temperance reformers legislate against the things which make for drunkenness, and do away with factories where, as Dr. Bellew of St. Helens said, "the men cannot work unless they are half-drunk."[1] For it is indeed rather on account of the physical exigencies of their work than because of the feeling of moral degradation that these people, as a class, exceed and are intemperate. Look at the nail-makers of Bromsgrove, who are the worst paid of all the white slaves. I never heard of a single instance of a man's "going on the beer" during all the days I spent in that picturesque but wicked little town. But then their work is not done in great heat; they do not stream with perspiration as they wield their hammers, and can eat and enjoy such miserable provender—one can hardly call it food—as they can afford out of their pitiful wages. And the same may be said of the slipper-makers. None of these people wish to drink; they drink because they cannot help themselves. They go as fatally to intemperance as Tess went

---

[1] See chapter on "The Chemical Workers."

PREFACE

to the gallows, under the whip of circumstance. As to the nail-makers in particular, they are no doubt in part also restrained by their sincere piety. This I describe in the chapter devoted to their mournful lives. One might search the British Isles from end to end, no truer Christians could be found than these poor men and women, whose hopes are not of this world, who derive courage and draw contentment from the promise of the hereafter. In their simplicity, in their faith and trust, they are as the little children to whom the Kingdom of Heaven was promised.

The exploration of the factories was an easy task. One had often but to walk confidently in at the front door with firm steps and a brazen forehead. Where this was impracticable there was the wall at the back. And there were other ways and means, which need not be detailed, lest helpful friends be molested. Mr. Piffard, the artist, who accompanied me, in every case applied to the masters for permission to visit the works. He could do this without *lèse*-hospitality, for his drawings were to be from nature, exact reproductions of things seen. In every case but one this permission was granted. The exception was at Widnes, where, at the office of the United Alkali Company, he was told that strangers could not be allowed to visit any of the works on any pretext whatever. So on this occasion he was forced to follow my example, and get over the wall at the back, or we should have had to do without his admirable pictures of the chemical workers. Of these pictures, I wish to say this, that in all the criticisms I have read of the articles exception has been taken to one only, and that is the picture illustrating a female woolcomber, who, suffering from the intense heat, has stripped herself to the waist.

Said Mr. Whitehead, of the Bradford Chamber of Commerce:[1] "As to the women workers, the statements with reference to them were not correct, and many of the women were very much annoyed at the sketch which was published with the article. He (Mr. Whitehead) had never heard of anything of the sort in the trade before, and it

[1] See Appendix. Report of Meeting of Bradford Chamber of Commerce.

was certainly not done at any of the large establishments." The picture was, no doubt, as true a reproduction of a thing seen as are all Mr. Piffard's drawings, of which I can only say that they do not perhaps illustrate the very worst aspects of these lives. Would the Bradford woolcombers (masters) have preferred our giving a picture of the scene where a girl fell down on the floor of a combing shed in the pains of labour, prematurely brought on by exhaustion?[1]

As to criticism, I am happy to say that on no single point of any importance have I received contradiction. The Widnes people were very indignant at my statements about the vegetation in and around their town, and some correspondents endeavoured to crush me under fine cabbages and trees in pots, which, living contradiction of my statements, were to be seen by all who had eyes to see. And that is about all. The newspapers in the towns which I have visited have almost all written favourably about my articles.

[1] This took place shortly before our visit to Bradford. The girl was taken home in a cab, but was delivered of a child on the way.

"It makes one shudder to read of the horrors suffered by these lead-workers," says the *Newcastle Leader*, which, had I exaggerated or misrepresented facts, would surely have been the first to point this out. And this is but one instance out of scores. For the rest, those who wish to read what contradictions have been made will find them in the appendix to this volume, where I have printed what seemed to me worthy of notice, however erroneous and unfounded I may know these contradictions to be. Now and again some bluster about proceedings in libel has been made, but to my intense disappointment nothing has ever come of this talk. I could wish for nothing better than to put into the witness-box a dozen ragged, starveling men and women to swear to the truth of every word I have written. It would cause some sensation in the law courts, and would serve our ends better than very many writings.[1]

Many people have said, commenting on

---

[1] Since the above was written I have myself been forced to take action against one newspaper which described me as "a liar, a base slanderer, and a sensation-mongering traducer."

what is written about women, that these are amply protected by the Factory Acts. " Oh, are they?" has been my invariable answer. If there is one Act of Parliament in existence through which it is easy to drive a coach-and-four it is the Factory Act. How, for instance, does it protect women—nailmakers, chainmakers, tailoresses, and so on—who work, not in factories, but in premises rented by themselves?

This misuser of women and children, indeed, is what is most revolting in all this mournful story. Could not something be done in this year of grace, in which the British Empire is preparing to celebrate the long life and glorious reign of a Sovereign Lady— Queen and Woman—to honour womanhood by rescuing from such nameless misery and degradation the thousands of that Lady's subjects, the thousands of women and girls who are oppressed because—being women— they are weak?

ROBERT HARBOROUGH SHERARD.

AUTHORS' CLUB,
3, WHITEHALL COURT, LONDON, S.W.
February 15th, 1897.

Original Preface

THE collection of material for this series of articles on the worst paid and most murderous trades of England occupied me for nearly two months in the spring of last year. During this period I visited six manufacturing centres in the Northern and Midland counties of England, spending about ten days in each district.

My time was passed almost entirely in the society of the workmen, at their clubs, in the public-houses which some frequent, in the workhouses to which nearly all come, in the hospitals, and in the workshops, which are the ante-rooms of the hospital and the workhouse.

I visited their cottages and conversed on questions of domestic economy with their wives, learning from the lips of these by what prodigies of management they could contrive to feed, clothe, and house their children, their husbands, and themselves, out of the irregular pittances which these deathly trades afford to the workers, comparing everywhere the statements of these and those, in an ardent quest of truth.

I visited the doctors in each town, and examined the books from which the *ægrotats* are delivered, as well as—kindest books for any who love the class to read—those in which the certificates of death stand copied.

On some occasions, just as the visitor to Dartmoor tastes the prison fare, I accepted their spontaneous offers of hospitality, taking "soops of yale" out of the common mug of the woolcombers of Bradford, or sharing in a solitary bowl of milkless tea with the "blue-bed women" of Newcastle-on-Tyne.

I avoided contact with the masters as far as possible, and am in no way indebted to any of them for assistance in my enterprise. The factories I visited were visited by me as a trespasser, and at a trespasser's risk. That, in conversations with employers in luxurious smoking-rooms, these should laugh at the stories of grievances which I related, is in the natural order of things.

Mr. Harold Piffard, the artist, who accompanied me, being in no way responsible for the things I was to set down, or for my manner of setting them down, worked on a different line. He visited the factories by the front door, where I had to climb over the wall at the back.

R. H. SHERARD.

I
The Alkali Workers

I

The Alkali Workers

WIDNES and St. Helens, where are situated the principal works in the alkali industry, are at all times the most dreary of places. Their especial ugliness is, however, never more marked than when the spring is making beautiful every nook and corner of England, for the spring never comes hither. It never comes because, neither at Widnes nor at St. Helens, is there any place in which it can manifest itself. The foul gases which, belched forth night and day from the many factories, rot the clothes, the teeth, and, in the end, the bodies of the workers, have killed every tree and every blade of grass for miles around.

In the old days, before the alkali works were established in Widnes, this town was known as Wood-end; nor is it very, very long ago since quite a pleasant bit of wood stood where now a muddy waste extends its dismal, swamp-like surface for hundreds of yards to the left of the railway embankment.

Now, except on the heights of Appleton, where the churchyard is, and where a careful farmer has coaxed some grass into being, there is no green anywhere—not one touch on which to rest the eye weary of blackish brown, and brownish black, of soot and mud, and the foul slimes thrown up by the sewers or set down by the poisoned air.

So malodorous is this wood-end town that, when the south wind is blowing, its obnoxious presence makes itself felt many miles away. Windows are closed, vinaigrettes are brought out, and evil things are said of the south wind, for all that it comes, fragrant till Widnes, from the orange-groves of Spain and the mimosa and violets of France. For miles round the poisonous air kills and kills, and so frequent are the

THE ALKALI WORKERS 49

claims for compensation made by neighbouring farmers for their acid-eaten crops against the factory owners, that these have found it a matter of economy to buy up the land in the sphere of influence of their sulphuretted hydrogen and other gases.

Trees cannot live here, but men must and do. Widnes is a populous town, and one admires in its squalid courts and alleys the swarms of healthy children.

"They are a fine race of men and women," said an informant, "and their children are beautiful."

One sees numerous and fine children, but rarely any old people amongst the alkali workers. The touching contrast between May and December will be looked for in vain in Widnes, for here, as in St. Helens, as the leading doctor in the latter town remarked to me, "the men go off quick."

"It is a very unhealthy trade," he said; "and if the published statistics show but a small death-rate in the chemical trade, it is because the chemical yard only kills a man three parts out of four, leaving the workhouse to do the rest. The men are dismissed before they are actually dying. As a general rule, the men go from forty-five to fifty-five years of age. The tubes become blocked up and asthmatical; the gases destroy all elasticity of the tubes. The lime-men get soft stone. All get more or less anæmic. Asthma, kidney disease, chronic cystitis are the perquisites of many."

In answer to a question the doctor said: "It would not be wise to pass a chemical-yard man at the ordinary rate for life insurance. The work certainly shortens life. For one thing, the men cannot do their work unless they are half-drunk. They drink and drink. I have one patient who drinks a half-cask (eighteen gallons) of beer a week. They drink because they cannot eat. I know men who have brought their breakfasts, dinners, and teas back home from the works, because they could not touch them. A man cannot be healthy under these conditions."

As to this excessive drinking, we shall hear more farther on. *En passant* I may remark that having quoted Dr. Bellew's remarks to one of the alkali workers in

THE ALKALI WORKERS 51

Widnes, he laughed, and said that a half-cask a week wouldn't be of much use to *him*. He was a salt-cake man, and he reckoned he did not have his allowance unless he had from twenty to thirty pints a day. He chuckled at the thought of a kilderkin a week for a thirsty salt-cake man, and showed his toothless gums.

There are nine doctors in Widnes, and there is work for them all amongst the men. The oldest practitioner in the town is Dr. O'Keefe, who has attended the chemical works in his capacity as doctor to the Mersey Chemical Works Club for upwards of thirty-one years.

It was thanks to his efforts and repeated applications to the Government that about four years ago a stop was put to the too liberal diffusion of sulphuretted hydrogen gas, which was slowly poisoning the people in the town. That it still breathes its lethal breath over Widnes may be seen in the large patches of metallic bluish green slime which cover the muddy expanses here and there. A walk down Snig Lane at four o'clock in the morning, when the factories let off the gas, would edify those who have heard that no deleterious gases are allowed to escape; whilst townspeople, not workers, can be found, who have had to leave their beds at this hour and rush out into the air, lest they should be suffocated. But the nuisance has certainly been diminished.

"It is a terribly poisonous gas," he said, "and but one of several which in these alkali works shorten life. There is this, however, to be said in its favour, that if it poisons men it poisons microbes also, and its effect is to minimise contagion by fever. We have but three patients at present in the fever hospital."

Apart from this admission in favour of this particular poison, Doctor O'Keefe's opinion on the work in the chemical factories is that it materially shortens life. "Very few men indeed," he said, "get above sixty."

A glance through the counterfoils of the book from which he delivers certificates of sickness to the workers was instructive. Of lumbago, caused by the terrible draughts

THE ALKALI WORKERS

in the factories, there were numerous cases; of gastralgia, many also, as of sciatica and influenza. But it was bronchitis, bronchial asthma, and bronchial catarrh that recurred with most frequency; lung diseases generated and fostered by the great heat of the furnaces in men exposed almost simultaneously to the icy cold of the ill-covered, ill-closed works.

As a burner said to me, " When you are working, you have one half of your body in the North Pole and the other half in Hell."

The certainty of a shortened life, the possibility of a sudden and terrible death, and constant risks of painful accidents are well known to all the chemical workers in these alkali factories, and are accepted by them with an indifference which might seem callous were it not so apparently heroic. The men joke about their condition.

I asked one man, whom I met in one of the factories, what they were manufacturing there.

" Skeletons," he said; " and I, you see, am only half-done."

The cemeteries where the workers are buried are at Appleton and at Wiston, and it is amongst the men a standing pleasantry to say that if these were dug up they would supply the raw material for a chemical yard. "You could get tons of alkali out of their bones and vats of acid." And the laugh goes round.

But Roger is their best joke, as Roger is their worst enemy. Roger is the chlorine gas, which, pumped on to slaked lime, transforms this into bleaching powder. Roger is a green gas, and is so poisonous that the men (packers) who pack the bleaching powder after the process into the barrels in which it is exported work with goggles on their eyes and twenty thicknesses of flannel over their mouths, these muzzles being tightly secured by stout cords. They can pack but a few minutes at a time. A "feed" of this gas kills its man in an hour.

For all that, Roger is the butt, not the bogey. True, that at the cry, "Roger is coming! Clear, lads!" so frequently heard in the works, a wild *sauve qui peut* of panic-stricken men may be seen scurrying before a green, perceptible, and palpable

COSTUME OF A BLEACHING POWDER PACKER.

fog borne on the wind, but all the same, once the danger is past, Roger evokes smiles.

"Why, the other day, sir," a packer tells me, "there was a man came with a donkey and a cart, and was standing with it close to the packing chamber, when he hears a cry of 'Roger is coming!' and naturally runs away. When he gets back he finds that the green fog has killed his donkey. That donkey died manfully." The last words raise a shout of laughter.

"Aye, Roger killed the donkey," says one.

"Yes, and the donkey died manfully," says another.

And they laugh and laugh, and forget the men he has killed, and will kill, it may be, amongst themselves.

A man who was just about to put on his muzzle to enter the packing-room in one of the factories, and thus about to face a terrible danger, tarried to tell me of an episode, humorous to his thinking, in which Roger had played a part.

"There was a cat used to come worriting round here," he said, "stealing our dinners and such like, and I wanted to get shut of him. So I collared him one day, and

THE ALKALI WORKERS 57

took him into the chamber and gave him a sniff. He was green in a second." And having spoken, he laughed heartily.

SLAIN BY "ROGER."

"Yes," added philosophically a comrade who was standing by, "and a cat has nine lives—a man only one."

The unpicturesqueness of Widnes is picturesque by the excess of its ugliness. It might have tempted Doré—one is sure it would have pleased Des Groux. Squalid cottages, large areas of muddy waste, with a pigstye here and there, and perhaps a gipsy's van in a desert of puddles and mud; black alleys, intricate gangways over an intricate network of railways, high chimneys on every side, and below these such grotesque shapes of towers and bubbling cauldrons, and tanks and wheels, as seem the very nightmare of industrialism.

There are open sewers, too, through which the green liquid refuse of factories is carried off, canals on which squat barges lie at anchor, and when the tide is out there may be seen by the great railway bridge which spans the Mersey a huge expanse of muddy sand. By this bridge, indeed, there are points from which the view just falls short of the picturesque—points at which, by contrast, one thinks of Venice, and in the grey lights grey Runcorn shows fantastic, the ugly city of an ugly dream, a mass of heaped-up masonries rising to the sky, mysterious, indefinite.

"THE FACTORIES, THOUGH SPACIOUS, ARE MEAN AND DIRTY.
THE APPROACHES SEEM TO BE RAILWAY SIDINGS."

(Page 61).

THE ALKALI WORKERS

Night, which makes all things beautiful, can lend no charm to Widnes. Doomed to ugliness, it has not that grandeur of factory towns, which at nights, at least, are fine, when every chimney in them is a flaming torch. The chimneys of Widnes do not flare. In all its effects it is petty and squalid. One looks in vain for the grandiose which gives to industrialism its artistic value.

The factories, though spacious, are mean and dirty. The approaches to them seem to be railway sidings; they appear to be huge sheds built over railway yards: sheds knocked together anyhow, with great holes in the roof and doorless entrances on every side. At these entrances may be seen on the railway lines, which envelope each factory as in a net, waggons and waggons of raw material—salt, sulphur-stone, slack, and other things which look like the refuse of the mineral world, but which here shall be transformed into yellow sulphur, bright copper, effulgent silver, and various chemicals whose chiefest use is to cleanse. Cleanliness out of filth, light out of darkness. If cleanliness be indeed next to godliness, then are these white slaves of Widnes pursuing a religious work.

Let us watch them at work. In little sheds down this long corridor are seated broken-down men, not old, but aged, breaking stones from which sulphur is to be extracted. These are technically known as the "stone nobblers," but, as Widnes will have its joke, they are more commonly called the "handbell ringers." They ring their bells the livelong day, and the music is paid at eightpence the ton. A king amongst stone nobblers can earn thirteen shillings a week, but few earn more than eight shillings.

"It's worse than on the high roads," said one, "but then you're warmer in the winter."

These men are the wasted alkali workers —toothless, asthmatic, half-blind, used up— "the cast-offs," as one man told me. He added, "This is the last stage before the workhouse."

The salt-cake men next. These play an important part. Under their hands common salt, baked in furnaces and treated

THE ALKALI WORKERS 63

with vitriol, produces, after various processes, hydrochloric acid gas, whence hydrochloric acid and chloride of manganese. The salt which remains in the furnace after the

A STONE NOBBLER (8d. THE TON).

hydrochloric acid has been drawn off is what is known as salt-cake.

Their work consists in spreading and turning the salt in the furnace, and in drawing it out when all the gas has been drawn off, for the most part through the high coke towers, where it is transformed by trickling water into liquid hydrochloric acid, and to some extent into their lungs, where it is transformed into death.

I had remarked to a man who was accompanying me that the works had not such an evil odour as I had been told, and he managed, by conspiracy with a salt-cake man, to give me a lungful of the gas, a joke that was practical and imparted direct information.

A salt-cake man can be recognised anywhere. His teeth, if not entirely destroyed, are but black stumps. The effect makes itself seen in under twelve months.

"It takes us longer to eat pap than it would a baby in the cradle," said one man.

Another, who was humorous, said: "Supposing I have to pay fifteen shillings a week for my tommy (food), I'll have to pay five shillings more to some one to gollop it for me."

By the side of one of the workers, strewed on the floor, I saw a quantity of crusts of bread. His teeth were too soft to eat them. "I'd have to soak 'em in my can before I could masticate them," he said; "and I've no time for that."

As a fact, these men, during their eight hours' daily work, can barely snatch a minute for their meals.

"We haven't a minute for a meal's meat," said one. "You have to eat like a dog. Standing at your work you eat your chuck."

A salt-cake man at St. Helens said: "My teeth are all gone. I have been at salt-cake for eighteen years. I have made twenty-four shillings a week at piece-work, working on Sundays—that is to say, seven shifts a week. If I wanted to keep Sunday, I shouldn't make a pound a week.

"I am standing eight hours on end in front of a fiery furnace, melting with heat, drawing, shoving, and turning the salt with an iron bar, which weighs fifty-six pounds. The heat is so intense that I am perspiring all the time. I have two towels to wipe myself on. One is drying whilst I am using the other. I eat only when I can snap. But I'm not often hungry, and the gas makes me sick. But I must stick to the furnace, or I'm going short of my wages." He added: "Not a man of my time but what is gone off or in the workhouse." He had lived for weeks on milk and eggs. "My stomach wouldn't stand anything solid." He has to drink to keep up his strength.

There is no Sunday, not even Christmas Day, for the alkali workers when trade is busy. At other times they have weeks and months of enforced idleness.

The eight hours day has been introduced into these works.

"They go swaggering about their eight hours," said one, "but they put more on us than before. We are working by the piece, and we punish ourselves to get our wages."

Mr. Healey, the secretary of the Chemical Workers' Union, said in this connection, "The men have to do twelve hours' work in eight hours."

Another salt-cake man in St. Helens had been recently discharged from the works for being an hour late one morning, after working steadily and without any loss of time for four months at this factory. He has been a salt-cake man for twenty years. "I overslept myself that morning and arrived at

seven instead of six. I was immediately discharged." He also said that it was often impossible for him to swallow any food, so that the fact that no time was allowed for meals was practically a matter of indifference. He added, "The only good thing for a man is a glass of summat."

The lime-men, or millers, are those who load the slaked lime, after turning it over and over, on to the lifts, by which it is conveyed to the chamber where it is treated with chlorine. These work in shifts of twenty minutes at a time, with a few minutes' interval for rest, for fourteen hours on the night shift, or for seven hours on the day shift.

It is dirty and dangerous work, with soft-stone as a certain perquisite and blindness as a possibility. So trifling a matter as large burns need not be referred to.

The men work with a thick oakum gag or "muzzle" in their mouths, in a cloud of white particles. In the summer the heat is quite intolerable. When they have done their work, they wash themselves with oil or tallow, and dry themselves on wisps of brown paper. This is all the toilet that they know. The use of water would flay them alive. They receive 1s. 3d. per ton, which is divided amongst nine in a gang, and their average wage is $3\frac{1}{2}d$. the hour. All the men are paid by tonnage, from the stone-nobblers up to the packers.

The mixers, who convey to the revolving burners, in bogeys, weighing loaded 50 cwt., stone, slack, or salt-cake, or from the burners the fiery black-ash, an average distance of 200 yards—at nights in almost total darkness—have an average wage of 3s. 9d. a day for eleven such journeys, besides loading and unloading. Usually two men run one such bogey, but I spoke to a man who had run a load of 3 tons 4 cwt., besides the weight of the car.

The packers, whose dangerous work and strange accoutrement have been described, receive two shillings per ton for turning and packing the poisonous bleaching-powder, and some can earn as much as fifty shillings a week. These men literally carry their lives in their hands. One hears of too many cases where "men got gas" and died within a few hours.

THE ALKALI WORKERS 71

"And it's almost always brought in accidental," said a packer, who was suspicious of the "crowner's" juries.

"Or," says another, "the master's doctor

"THESE MEN LITERALLY CARRY THEIR LIVES IN THEIR HANDS."

will say the man died of a faint. It's like this. You get gas. We run to the office for the brandy bottle and say, 'So-and-so's got gas.' Brandy is served out. You go home and die. Doctor says you died of faint, and the proof is that brandy was needed to revive you."

The vatmen, who convey the cooled black-ash into the vats where it is diluted in water, must push and unload forty barrows to fill one vat. Two vatmen can fill three vats in a day, working from eleven to eighteen hours. The pay is 2s. 8d. for each vat. The men have to go on their knees some part of the way to push the barrows along. The vatmen that I saw looked so draggled, so forlorn, so degraded, that I think that of all these poor fellows I pitied them the most.

Mr. Healey declared to me that, taking an average, the wages paid to the alkali workers to-day are fifty per cent. lower than they were five or six years ago, before the various masters syndicated their interests. On the other hand, the manufactures have in the same period notably advanced in price.

On December 28th, 1889, bicarbonate of soda was quoted at £5 5s. per ton. During my visit to Widnes it was quoted at £7 per ton. Salt-cake has advanced from 1s. to 2s., caustic soda from 2s. 6d. to 5s., whilst bleaching-powder, packed in hard wood barrels, which was quoted in 1889 at £5 10s. per ton, has advanced to £7 5s.

"NUMEROUS ARE THE STORIES OF MEN BOILED TO DEATH IN THE STEAMING CAUSTIC POTS."

Miserable as the wages are, earned at such risks and with such real physical exhaustion and suffering, the men would yet be contented could they rely on any regularity of work. But they cannot. They are the sport of the markets. Sometimes trade is so slack that they must loaf about idle for weeks and weeks.

One man told me that on an average he was working one week out of four. Some finishers said that during slack times they worked one week and idled the next. On the other hand, when the rush is on the men are allowed no breathing time—not a day's rest, little of the night, no Sunday, no Christmas.

This is their chief complaint—the uncertainty of their earnings. Of "Roger" and salt-cake gas, and the hundred other risks that attend them, they speak lightheartedly. Not long before my visit to Widnes, three men cleaning out one of the open sewers to which I have referred were asphyxiated, and numerous are the stories of men boiled to death in the steaming caustic-pots.

A mere walk through a yard is dangerous, for the tanks leak here and there, and corrosive fluids drop and drop. One hears of a man who was slowly eaten to death in a vitriol-tank into which he had fallen, and in which he was caught fast. A priest tried to reach him to anoint him, but failed. Hundreds, powerless to help, were looking on. He joked at them between his screams. " Were they all out on strike to be idling there?"

In Wiston Workhouse is a legless man, with whom an armless man keeps company. They were both alkali workers.

Yet ugly Widnes is a land of beer and beef. We have heard of the kilderkin man and of the man who was better at his beer than he. Butchers' shops abound, where prime joints are retailed at 2½d. the pound. In St. Helens I saw meat offered at 1½d. the pound, whilst in the market there on Saturday night I heard butchers crying: " Top price for everything—4d. !"

One wonders hów the workers can clothe themselves. They must wear wool, for the gas rots cotton in forty-eight hours. Men are seen going home with their breeches roped round their legs, because their garments were sewn with cotton, and the seams have given; or in a network of woollen woof, the cotton warp having disappeared. I saw one man clothed mainly with an old nitre-bag.

The last sight that horrible Widnes afforded to my eyes was not the least degrading. The Bench was sitting at the Town Hall, and from the Town Hall to the Railway Station the street was lined with those who were perforce idle. There were many women amongst the crowd, and some had children in their arms.

"What are these people waiting to see?" I asked of my companion. "They have the eager eyes and that stretching of their necks which betokens expectations."

"There's always a crowd," was the answer, "when the Bench is sitting. They're waiting to see the prisoners come out. The chaps what have been sent up to Liverpool to do a bit of time."

I was about to speak, when cries of "Here they come!" "Hurrah!" ran like a *feu de joie* down the thick lines. There were several prisoners. One was a woman. The prisoners at Widnes have to walk through

THE ALKALI WORKERS 77

the principal street of the town to the station. The men were handcuffed in couples. The mob gloated over the shackles. In slavery also there are degrees. The unfettered exult.

The thanks of Mr. Piffard and myself are due to Mr. Patrick Healey, secretary of the now disbanded Chemical Workers' Union, for the kind assistance he gave us during our visit to St. Helens and Widnes.

NOTE.—In the Appendix to this volume will be found certain hostile comments on the foregoing article, to which the reader is referred.

II

The Nailmakers of Bromsgrove

II

The Nailmakers of Bromsgrove

THE sadness of the lives of the nailmakers of Bromsgrove and district is accentuated by the fact that there, at least, unlike the murky towns which have been described, there are many simple, natural things which would make even a poor life happy, given a humble and contented nature, such as is the prime characteristic of these workers. The little town is bright and sweet and clean, with many picturesque old houses and a fine old church, and all round it, within two minutes' walk from the long, principal street, is some of the prettiest country in the Midlands: trees and meadows and brooks and undulating slopes, with lovers' lanes for long walks to many sites, historical and picturesque.

A simple man, a God-fearing man—and the Bromsgrove nailmaker is both God-fearing and simple—might be very happy here, where what is best in town and country

SOME OF THE BROMSGROVE NAILMAKERS.

is combined, did not an imminent and terrible danger at all times overcast his life with the blackest of shadows; the imminent and terrible danger called clamming. Now, the plain English for clamming is starvation.

"Nailmaking," said to me Mr. J. Powell, formerly secretary of the now disbanded Nailmakers' Union, "is one of the worst trades in the kingdom. There are scores of men in this parish who are not earning nine shillings a week for seventy, eighty, or ninety hours' work, and out of these earnings have to pay from one shilling to eighteenpence a week for firing, and about sixpence for keeping their tools in order."

On investigation the fact becomes patent that in this idyllic scene is laid the action of one of the cruellest industrial tragedies in England, a tragedy all the more poignant because the sufferers are simple, defenceless men, admirably yet pitifully resigned, who would be very happy with very little, the little which, in spite of unceasing, lifelong toil, they are never able to obtain.

The industry of nailmaking is profitable only to those who do not make them; to this the luxurious houses and carriages of the nailmasters eloquently testify. And to become a nailmaster requires neither knowledge, nor brains, nor capital. Anybody with a few pounds to start with can enter this business, for success in which apparently nothing is needed except an entire absence of the altruistic sense. All that has to be done is to rent a small warehouse, to purchase a weighing machine, and to engage at, say, fourteen shillings a week a man to look after the warehouse, weigh the nails, and keep the accounts.

A little writing of business letters at home and an occasional trip to neighbouring markets will keep the nailmaster pleasantly employed. The nailers will do all the rest. They will find the workshops, the tools, the firing, and even the iron, and each week will bring the nails to the warehouse to be weighed and paid for. There is no risk, and there is a certain profit, because for certain classes of nails there is a steady and increasing demand.

Formerly the masters used to supply the bundles of iron to the workers, receiving them back in the form of nails, and allowing for a certain amount of waste

THE NAILMAKERS 85

(about 14 lbs. to each bundle of 60 lbs.) Now it is customary to refuse to a would-be-worker the advance of even one bundle, so that unless he can find the 3s. 6d. necessary for its purchase, he must just forego

THE NAILMAKERS' COTTAGES.

nailing. And there are hundreds of men and women in the Bromsgrove district who never have 3s. 6d. to lay out in advance from one year's end to another.

"We have to buy our iron at 3s. 6d. the bundle," said a woman to me; "and after we have worked one in, they give we another out."

But they never advance the first bundle. Speaking of this hardship, one woman told of better days long past.

"In them days," she said, "we usen't to have to stand still for want of iron. Nowadays, at most factories, it's: 'You won't get no iron here.' Why, they wouldn't trust you for a bundle of iron, not if you clammed a week."

To each cottage in Bromsgrove, Sidemoor, and the district is attached a nailing shed, the rent for which is included in that of the cottage. Each of these sheds is fitted with a forge and bellows, provided by the landlord. The nailer has to find his own bench and set of tools, at an outlay of from five to ten pounds.

The bench is fitted with a peg, or miniature anvil, on which the red-hot iron is pointed; a hardy, or fixed chisel, over which the iron is bent and partially cut; a bore, into which the severed length is inserted previous to the fashioning of the head of the nail. This is effected by means of the

THE NAILMAKERS 87

Oliver, which is a heavy hammer worked by a treadle, and restored to its upright

NO IRON.

position by a simple system of leverage. The completed nail is ejected from the bore by means of a lever, operating on a tit, or tiny steel rod, which, jerked upwards, expels the nail.

In some of the nailing sheds may be seen at work as many as four nailers, each provided with his bench. Of these one is the tenant of the shed, and the others are "stallers." The "stallers" are working, each on his own account, contributing to the rent and the firing. It is cheaper for them to co-operate in this manner than for each to rent his own shed and supply his own firing.

On the first day of my visit to Bromsgrove, I called on a number of nailers in the town itself. Off the principal street are numerous courts, and in each court may be found nailmakers' cottages, with nailmakers at work in adjoining sheds. Thus one can pass in one minute from prosperous burgherdom to the lowest slavery.

The first shed which I visited was in a not unpicturesque courtyard, not far from the beautiful church. A professional pig-sticker appeared to be the presiding genius

INTERIOR OF A BROMSGROVE NAILMAKER'S SHED, OCCUPIED BY
THE MAN AND TWO FEMALES, THE LATTER WORKING EACH
ON HER OWN ACCOUNT, AND PAYING 6d A WEEK RENT, AND
FINDING HER TOOLS — THE SPADE, THE HEAVY HAMMER,
THE OLIVER, THE BELLOWS ATTACHED TO THE HEARTH
AND THE LIGHT HAND VICE.

THE NAILMAKERS 91

of the place, and, if I refer to this, it is because, as will later transpire, the professional pig-sticker is to the nailmakers the one streak of silver lining in their black and heavy cloud. There were three men at work in this shed, the tenant and two stallers, who paid 6d. a week stalling apiece, and one third of the firing, the weekly cost of which was 2s. 6d.

The persistent laboriousness of these men was my first impression. Not for one second did they interrupt their mechanical movements, undisturbed by our advent, indifferent to all but the maximum to be effected. They answered my questions, they even made comments, but their weary eyes never deflected from their work, their hands and feet busy in one monotonous jig. Now it was working the bellows, now stoking the fire, now turning the irons, and now fashioning them on the bench—a series of brusque, jerky, harassed movements, not for one second suspended; perpetual motion, under the whip of hunger, as long as nerves could direct and muscles fulfil.

These men were making Flemish tacks;

and one of them, speaking for all, told me that even by working fifteen hours a day he could not earn 12s. a week. "Out of this I have to pay stalling and breeze" (the name given to the firing). To earn 12s. a week he would have to make over 20,000 Flemish tacks, and that was beyond his powers. He could make 20,000 Flemish tacks in one week, but not more.

It is necessary to remark that, by a pleasant little custom of the trade, a thousand nails, as between man and master, are twelve hundred nails, but only eight hundred (especially in the matter of hobnails) as between master and customer. Result, four hundred nails gratis in the warehouse.

Thus, 20,000 Flemish tacks means 24,000. Each 1000 (1200) tacks is paid for with $6\frac{1}{2}d$.

"The right price on them," said the man, "is $7\frac{1}{2}d.$, but we is paid $6\frac{1}{2}d.$ because we've nothing to do."

This man admitted his inability to make more than twenty thousand (24,000) of these nails in one week. His work would consequently produce $20 \times 6\frac{1}{2}d. = 10s.\ 10d.$

From this he would have to deduct 6*d*. for stalling and 9*d*. for breeze, leaving (10*s*. 10*d*. – 1*s*. 3*d*.) 9*s*. 7*d*. Thus, for making 24,000 tacks he would receive 9*s*. 7*d*., less 6*d*. for wear and tear of his tools, leaving 9*s*. 1*d*. This means that he has to make 220 tacks for 1*d*.

The manufacture of each tack involves, besides the accessories of working the bellows, turning the irons, and stoking, the following labour: The red-hot iron is laid on the peg, and with from four to six blows of the hand-hammer, whilst the rod is turned with the other hand, the point of the nail is fashioned. The now pointed bar is laid on the hardy, the point touching a gauge by which the length of the nail is regulated. A blow with the hand-hammer cuts the nail-length almost off the bar and bends it, thus almost severed, at right angles.

This length is now inserted in the bore; the cold iron is twisted away from it, and with a movement of the foot Oliver is brought down, flattening the protruding mass and forming the head of the tack. Sometimes Oliver has to be brought down twice, and usually, at least, two blows with the hand-hammer are necessary to properly fashion the head. Then the lever ejecting the nail from the bore has to be worked. This completes the operation.

Allowance must also be made for time lost in welding together the fag-ends of the iron rods, when these become too short to be handled, as also in case the blow on the hardy entirely detaches the red-hot point, when it has to be picked up and inserted in the bore by means of a pair of nippers. On the other hand, as the men always work two rods at the same time, a little time is saved in the matter of bellows-blowing, turning, and stoking, although each tack exacts the separate and repeated operations described. These operations have to be carried out 220 times in their entirety to earn the wage of 1d.

Flemish tacks can, I believe, be made by machinery, but this cannot be said of brush nails, which were being made by a cadaverous-looking man in the next shed visited. Brush nails are bought at the warehouses at

THE NAILMAKERS

1s. 3½d. the thousand (1200), and this man was earning 7s. a week at the making of them. He works from 7 a.m. till 10 p.m.,

"SEVEN SHILLINGS A WEEK."

and turns out about 11 lbs. of these nails in a week.

"I could make more if I were stouter," he said, "but I got ill by clamming and going short on my belly."

He was paying 8*d*. a week for stalling and 1*s*. 2*d*. a cwt. for breeze.

"I pays more than I burns," he said.

It was a very draughty shed, and the man coughed terribly.

In the next place there were working side by side an old man of sixty and his wife. The shed was filled with poultry: hens were roosting over the forge, hens were brooding in packing-cases in the corners. The man had been at the trade all his life, and said:

"It's never been worse in price."

He was making clout nails at 8¼*d*. for 3¼ lbs. He could make about 30 lbs. in a week, and could earn at it about 7*s*. His wife made tacks at 6*d*. the 1000, and could earn about 1*s*. a day, working nine hours.

I begged a few words of her. She told me that formerly, "when nailing was better, we made 20*s*. a week between us. My old man has told you the outside farthing that he earns. His average is 6*s*. 3*d*. a week, and when Saturday comes it is hard to lay it out. I have to turn it over very often. And my old man is the hardest-working man in

THE NAILMAKERS

Bromsgrove, and has never been on the beer in his life."

Out of their wages she had to pay 2s. 6d. a week rent for cottage and workshop, 1s. for repair of tools, and 1s. 1d. for fuel. Tea, bread, and margarine were the staple food; bread and cheese were an occasional treat; sixpennyworth of meat came once a week.

Clothes were out of the question.

"I has been married twenty-three years," she said, "and I has never had a new dress since I were married. Amusement?" she added. "There is none for me; bed and work is all we get."

This woman has brought up six children.

Amongst the lamentable documents which I brought home with me from Bromsgrove I find a written statement showing how a nailer, his wife, and five children live on the 15s. a week which by their joint efforts the parents can earn.

This is the budget: Rent, 2s. 6d.; firing, 1s. 6d.; repair of tools and kitchen fuel, 1s. 6d.; bread, 4s. 6d.; bacon, 9¾d.; meat, 9d.; margarine, 1s.; cheese, 5d.; sugar, 7d.; tea, 4½d.; tobacco, 3d.; lamp-oil, 2d.; candles,

1¼d.; soap, 3d.; sundries, 3½d. Sundries may be supposed to include such luxuries as clothing, milk, potatoes, literature, amusements, doctor, medicines, and so on.

A sad case was that of an old man, all alone in his shed, who told me he worked from 6 a.m. to 10 p.m. to earn 10s. a week. To avoid repetition, it should be understood that the wages mentioned are in each case to be taken as subject to the deductions for rent, breeze, and repair of tools. Whilst sedulously working he remarked:

"You can't earn what you ought to have to eat. It's one of the disgracefullest of trades."

He has been many a time on the parish because he could not get a living. In the summer, he said, with twinkling eyes, he has occasional "fine times." This is when he can get damsons to pick at 10d. the pot. He can pick as many as three and a half pots in sixteen hours. He was never a drinker, and has brought up a family of six children. His wife is a cripple, and "hasn't brought me in a ha'penny for fifteen years."

DELIVERING THE NAILS AT THE FACTORY.

"A thousand nails, as between man and master, are twelve hundred nails, but only eight hundred (especially in the matter of hobnails) between master and customer. Result, four hundred nails gratis in the warehouse." *See page 92.*

THE NAILMAKERS 101

He has four meals a day, and allows himself five minutes for each meal—that is to say, twenty minutes out of the sixteen hours. On feast days he may get a bit of "stupid" (bacon) to his dinner, but usually it's bread and tea-kettle broth which compose his menu.

"The kittle have to go on most times," he said.

This man was making a variety of nails, known as "improved fitters," and seemed keenly actuated with a desire for an improvement in the fitness of things, the nail trade included.

Were it not for their poultry and what they can earn as agricultural labourers in the summer, the nailmakers would undoubtedly starve. However, what with a pig (reared either in the shed or the kitchen, à la mode d'Irlande) and fowls and ducks, and odd jobs on the neighbouring farms in the season, they manage during the fine weather to save a pound or two to help them over the winter.

I then came upon an unhappy family hammering away for dear life. There were the father, the mother, the son and the daughter. The shed was dark but for the glare of the forge. The father said that all together "we don't get up to 13s. a week." I should explain that the daughter was a child of three, who was sitting on the forge, warming her naked little toes at the comfortable blaze, and hammering them in pure enjoyment on the brick-laid hearth, and that the son, a lad of about thirteen, who had passed the sixth standard, could only ".do a few nails after school-time," perhaps 2000 (2400) a week, and earn 10d. The mother said that often on Saturdays, after all debts were paid, she had not one shilling "to go to town with to buy a bit of meat for Sunday's boiling." As to clothes, she had had two new dresses since she was married, sixteen years ago, and one of these was thanks to a subscription which was raised at her chapel, when she buried her eldest child, and a black dress seemed necessary.

Next door I found a man of about sixty-five, who had been working at the trade for fifty years, and, without interruption, from 7 a.m. till 10 p.m. per diem. He couldn't earn a shilling a day and "mostly earned ten-

THE NAILMAKERS 103

pence." His aged mother and another old man were working in the same shop. Each nail that he made involved two blows with the Oliver, and three with the hand-hammer.

As we were returning from Sidemoor that evening, Mr. Powell told me of the malpractices of the "fogger." The fogger is the middleman, usually a small store-keeper, who flourishes in the Bromsgrove district in spite of the Truck Act and Her Majesty's Commissioners for Oyer and Terminer. He contracts with the masters to supply such quantities of nails, and obtains these nails from the makers at about 30 per cent. less than the tariff price.

He pays for the nails, sometimes in money, but more often in goods from his shop— bread, iron, breeze, and so on—which he sells at, at least, 30 per cent dearer than the non-fogging tradesmen of the town. But then he gives credit. He is liable to the penalties of the Truck Act, no doubt, but, as Mr. Powell says, the men dare not give evidence against him. One fogger was, however, recently prosecuted by Mr. Powell and heavily fined.

Amongst the many sad and haggard faces which the mere name of Bròmsgrove evokes, I think the one that haunts me most is that of a very old man, with whom I conversed on the last morning of my stay in that idyllic town. He was a man of eighty-five, who started nailing at the age of seven. His memory was quite clear. He had worked at the trade for seventy-seven years, and only " giv' over " a year come Whitsuntide, because, though working six or seven hours a day, he could only earn 1s. 6d. (less 6d. for stalling) in the whole week. This was very much less than he earned before he was eight years of age, when, as he told me, he could make his 1s. a day, working from 7 a.m. till 8 p.m. " Times were then half as good again as now."

In his good days, when he was rearing his nine children, he was earning his £1 a week.

" Ay, there was grand times in nailing in those days. One took one's nails and had £1, and the masters gave you a bag to put nails in, and a white rubber to clean up your tools."

THE NAILMAKERS 105

"HE HAD WORKED AT THE TRADE FOR SEVENTY-SEVEN YEARS."

But, he admits, nailing has been going down steadily for forty years.

"It's the foggers ruins such as we," said

his daughter. "Ay, foggers charge such outdashus prices," said the old man. He added: "It's not because there's no work. It's because of the masters bantering the men so down that they can't get bread. I'se been flogged in my time by not having my earnings. One has a feather off it, another has another, and there's little of the goose left."

This fine old man has now been in receipt of parish relief, after seventy-seven years of strenuous labour, for twelve months.

I could cite a hundred cases almost as distressful, but my prescribed space allows only of a few general remarks. One grievance of the workers, a very comprehensible grievance, is that often a whole week's work is rejected at the warehouse, on one pretext or another, as unsatisfactory. Possibly the master has ordered more than he can place. The men have to bear the loss and toil back home under their parcels "to do the best they can" with the nails, to sell them for what they will fetch, as waste iron or otherwise. "Make soup of them!" was the answer given to a nailer by a nail master, in answer to a despairing cry. Again, even to earn a bare subsistence many men work all night for several nights in the week.

Yet, in spite of all these woes and worries, the Bromsgrove nailers are a contented, resigned, and God-fearing race.

"I'se thankful for what I gets," said an old man to me.

Another, at Sidemoor, said: "I have never had my wages here, but when I get to Heaven I shall get my reward, and my oppressor will get his. The workman is worthy of his hire, and I—I am living in the hopes of Heaven."

The Bible thrown into the scale makes their lot seem happy to these heroic Christians. As they toil at their anvils they sing hymns. The "Doxology" is a favourite anthem. The last sound I heard as I left Bromsgrove was the voice of a poor old woman, bowed and almost blind, who was working at her forge. She was singing in an enthusiasm of hope and fervour, "The Lord will provide."

III
The Slipper-Makers and Tailors of Leeds

III

The Slipper-Makers and Tailors of Leeds

THE slipper, that emblem of the domestic comfort and virtues, must appear to any one who has investigated the conditions under which it is manufactured an emblem also of oppression and misery. On leaving Leeds, after having carefully studied the slipper-making trade, I asked Mr. Coyle, who was at one time secretary of the now disbanded Slipper-makers' Union, and is himself one of the worst victims of this industry, to write me, in his own language, a letter detailing his grievances. I reproduce here the most salient passages from this "human document."

"In relation to slipper-making," he writes, "allow

me to state, in the first place, that at the best of times and under the most favourable conditions it could only be classed amongst the starved industries of the country, and the only saving clause was this : we had always plenty of work until the Russian Jew appeared on the scene, and then a rapid change set in. The reason of this great change is the unfair competition of the Jew.

"The classes of work that we receive 9s. per dozen for the Jew makes for 5s., and the class we receive 8s. for the Jew makes for 4s.; and that is our main trade, namely, women's patent leather slippers; and for men's patent leather slippers I receive 14s. per dozen, and the Jew will make them for 7s. 6d. So that the reason the Christian is out of work is not far to seek, and the reason they can do this is on account of the number of hours they work.

"It is no uncommon thing to see a Jew start work at 7 a.m. and work until midnight, and in these hours, with the assistance of a sticker, he will make from ten to twelve dozen pairs of indifferent slippers in a week.

"Now mark the difference. I contend that no man can make more than four pair of slippers in a day of nine hours and make them passable, and for this a man will receive the munificent sum of 3s.; that is wages with a vengeance for a skilled artisan, and even at that wage we cannot get sufficient work. And let me say, in conclusion, that if the general public really knew the above facts, there is not a man or a woman in the city but would feel ashamed to wear slippers made under such unfair conditions of labour. The monotony of a slipper life is dreadful in the extreme no time for recreation, no time for exercise of any description; off the seat and into bed; out of bed and on the seat again—a continual life of slavery."

It had taken me some time to find the writer of this letter, his circumstances forcing him to live in one of the worst parts of Leeds—namely, in a courtyard off the notorious High Street, which is never entered by the police except in couples. His cottage was one of the poorest I have yet seen—a two-roomed house, with a cellar, looking out on a brick wall about five feet from the window. There was little furniture in the downstairs room; the upstairs room served both as bedroom and workshop.

His manner was pitifully sad and depressed.

"I do feel the poverty of my house," he said. "I have had to sell my furniture piece-meal, to keep me and the lad alive. I once had a good home, for my wife was a house-proud woman." Working hard a full week for fourteen hours a day, he can earn, when there is work to do, about 13s. 9d., but he admits that he is not as strong as he used to be, that "he is going down the hill."

He added that he was less affected by constant physical suffering than by the humiliation of his position.

"It makes me miserable to be so badly paid," he said, "because it makes me feel that I am of no use in the world."

In a spirit of manly pride, which, however much political economy may blame it, I cannot but admire, he refuses to work below a certain minimum fixed by himself.

"I have often refused," he said, "to make men's slippers at 13*s.* the dozen, although the Jews make these at 7*s.* 6*d.* I would far rather go to the Union."

In Mr. Coyle's company, I visited a number of slipper factories, where foreign Jews are exclusively employed, and called on several Englishmen working in their miserable homes. The English workers have been almost entirely crowded out of the trade by the foreigners, and the few that remain are literally on the verge of starvation. On the other hand, there are over 1000 Jewish

A SLIPPER-MAKER'S HOME—PAST TEN AT NIGHT.

families of foreign extraction engaged in this industry in Leeds alone.

In the one downstairs room of a house in one of the lowest neighbourhoods in Leeds, I found an old slipper-maker at his tea. Although it was then past ten at night, his five little children were up and with him. As his wife explained:

"They've got to be there when there's something to eat going. Father chucks them a bit of bread now and again, and so they likes to be there."

It was a crowded scene, and one wondered how a man could live and work in such a room. Yet here this man had worked for thirty years, and never less than fourteen hours a day.

"Many a week," he said, "I have to work on Sundays also."

Most of Saturday is wasted, as on Saturdays he has to carry the week's work to the shop, to have it inspected and paid for. He declared that his life was a miserable one, and that the trade had never been worse.

"Work my very best, I can't earn 4d. an hour."

It was a good week with him when he earned 18s.; and out of this he had to pay 2s. 8d. for rent, and 9d. a week for findings. These findings would consist of paste (1½d.), hemp (6d.), sandpaper, ink, and white wax (1½d.).

He was a man naturally of a jovial temperament, which only made his misery show more lamentably. He showed me a neat pair of patent leather slippers which he had just finished.

"That shoe," he said, "will wear six Jew shoes. There's craft in that shoe; there's artisanship, there's work. We put 14d. worth of work in for 9d., to see if we can't win the trade back."

And he added that he had spent two hours thirty minutes in making these slippers. He would receive 9d. for this work. The slippers would be sold at retail for 3s.

He laughed when I asked him what pleasure he enjoyed in life.

"There's no such thing as pleasure for me. I go from my bed to my seat, and from my seat to my bed, though now and again I may get, say, an hour over my paper."

He laughed again when I asked him if he was able to save anything.

"Not a blessed halfpenny," he said; and his wife added that she could never

IN A JEW SLIPPER FACTORY.

make out how they managed to get along on his wages. She did the baking, and home baking was a comfortable thing. Some weeks she might get about 3d. worth of meat for the family dinner, but that was not often. Bread and tea were what they mainly lived on, and plenty of "working man's beef"—" that is to say, onions."

"There's grand stuff in onions," said this cheerful yet most unhappy man, who, in conclusion, told me that he meant to go on working his hardest until he could work no more, and that then, he supposed, they would find room for him in the workhouse.

An impressive sight was that of a number of foreign Jews working in a slipper factory at close upon eleven o'clock at night. At the far end of an immense room, the floor of which was strewn with *débris* of every kind, were a number of low, round tables, covered with tools, cardboard soles, leather tops, paste-jars, and similar objects. In the centre of each table flared a bright naphtha light.

Round each table sat three or four men stitching, or hammering, or pasting, with such rapidity that it was impossible to follow their movements. Dozens of completed slippers lay on the floor, a certain number—and such a number!—round the feet of each man, representing his day's work.

These men had been working just as I saw

THE SLIPPER-MAKERS 121

them work since 8 a.m., and did not expect to be through till past midnight.

"And the people going down Lady Lane," said one of them, grinning and nodding his head in the direction of the window, "and seeing the windows of the factory lighted up at past midnight, will say, 'There's them Jews making money,'" at which all laughed.

It was easy to understand their amusement at this sally when it transpired that the "top of the tree" remuneration for work so rapid and continuous was 4d. the hour, and that but very few of them could make as much, because 4d. was the price paid for a finished pair of slippers, and none but the very best worker could finish a whole pair of slippers in one hour. Yet one of these men, whose hands went and came with lightning rapidity, and who never paused a second whilst he was talking to me, admitted that he could finish twelve or thirteen pair of slippers, at 4d. the pair, in a day, working from fourteen to seventeen hours. This man said that in some weeks he had earned as much as 30s.

The work consists in cutting out the soles, cutting the cardboard false soles, pasting these in, attaching them to the leather sole, sewing this to the tops, which are supplied ready, lining and finishing the slipper ready for the retail shop. The tops are sewn and fitted with toe-caps by women, who work with machinery, and are paid 1$s.$ the dozen. This is for outside work.

Women engaged in the factories work by time, and earn about 12$s.$ a week, working from 7.30 to 6.30. They are expected to turn out as much as if working by the piece, and enough over and above to recoup the owner of the factory for his expenses in supplying steam power.

Few men earn anything like the wages mentioned in connection with the Lightning Slipper-maker. Most of the men to whom I spoke told me that, working as hard as they could, they could not get 3$d.$ the hour. The men work in twos in the factory; one sews, the other does the rest. The sewer earns about 16$s.$ for sewing ten dozen pair of slippers, so that his wages barely exceed 2$d.$ the hour.

The Jews do not work on the Sabbath, nor do they work during Passover, because, by

FITTING TOE-CAPS TO SLIPPER-TOPS.

their religion, they may not, during that festival, touch the paste which is used in slipper-making, for it contains leaven.

When I left this factory it was just midnight, and the men were working away as hard as ever. I felt very sorry for them, and could not help admiring their marvellous skill and industry. But I also felt very sorry for the unhappy Englishmen, whose bread they have taken. During the last few years, in which time the foreigners have almost entirely appropriated this trade, more than 250 English slipper-makers in Leeds alone have "gone under."

A few are in the workhouse, where I spoke to a poor old man of seventy-five, who had worked at the trade all his life, and had once been fairly prosperous, some have committed suicide, many have totally disappeared. An impoverished employer of labour told me that whereas some years ago, before the Jewish immigration, he had found work for upwards of 200 Englishmen, he could now only employ five men.

In comparison to the slipper-makers, the tailors and tailoresses of Leeds—and they themselves admit it—have a prosperous time; yet investigation proves that they also work under conditions akin to slavery,

THE SLIPPER-MAKERS 125

both in respect of the tyranny to which they are subjected and the totally inadequate remuneration which they receive. One of the chief complaints of the men refers to the abominable quality of much of the cloth which is given to them to work into clothes.

"This cloth," said a cutter to me, "is made of anything and everything except cast-iron. It is sized with manure, so that when we put the iron to it we get choked with stinking gas."

This extraordinary statement was afterwards confirmed to me by a Yorkshire squire, whom I met at Newcastle, and who told me that in his district large quantities of pig manure were purchased annually by the cloth manufacturers who supply the Leeds tailoring firms, for sizing the cloth.

The cutter added that string, cork, feathers, wire, and stones are found in quantities in this kind of cloth, and that when the circular steam-driven knife, with which twenty, thirty, forty, or fifty double thicknesses of cloth are cut out according to the pattern chalked on the top piece, comes into contact with either stone or wire, the danger of its breaking is very great.

"And when one of these endless band knives does break, as happens very often, you never know where it's going to fly to."

This particular man was not dissatisfied with his wages. He was in a good shop, he said, and made 30s. a week for seventy hours' work. But he complained of the exhausting nature of his employment.

"It's very heavy work pulling fifty double thicknesses of cloth under the knife," he said, "and men as good as me are only earning 24s. a week at that game, and some much less."

He told me that the cutters at a notorious sweating shop were only receiving 18s. a week, for twelve hours' work a day.

"The cloth is something diabolical," he said. "I never can wear a watch in the factory, because the dust from the cloth gets into it; so you can be sure it gets into the lungs. If I hang my coat up, it's covered with muck in two hours."

He was responsible for any damage done to cloth so rotten that "if you give it a pull, it comes to pieces"—cloth " that you can stick your finger through."

There are upwards of 4000 Jewish families engaged in the tailoring trade in Leeds, and these have all arrived there during the

" WHEN ONE OF THESE ENDLESS BAND-KNIVES DOES BREAK, YOU NEVER KNOW WHERE IT'S GOING TO FLY TO."

last fifteen years. The numbers increase annually; last year 100 families immigrated from Poland. A gentleman who knows the trade told me that the condition of the Jewish tailors in Leeds was fairly satisfactory. They themselves paint it in roseate hues.

I visited the Club of the Jewish Tailors' Union, in Regent Street, in the notorious Leylands, a club which occupies a room which was once a Baptist chapel. I endeavoured to obtain information from various members, but their prudence was extreme. They were all very comfortable, they said, earning splendid wages, and they mentioned as their weekly earnings sums which they did not obtain in a month. Rumours of anti-Jewish immigration laws have disturbed them, and they do not know what to say.

But from what I saw in the sweating dens in the Leylands, I am convinced that their circumstances are, at least, as bad as those of the sweated tailors in London. They all work on a weekly wage, and from twelve to seventeen hours a day. Here may be seen, in some filthy room in an old dilapidated factory in the Leylands, fifty people (men, women, boys, and girls), all huddled together, sewing as though for dear life. A girl may be earning 6s. a week, a man from 22s. to 30s. The stench in the room, its uncleanliness, surpass description. The finished

THE SLIPPER-MAKERS 129

garments are lying pell-mell on the floor in the filth and the vermin.

They are "flogged into their work," as

"THE GAUNT SWEATER STALKS ABOUT SCOLDING."

one said, "for all the time the gaunt sweater stalks about, scolding, inspecting, while now and then he will snatch a garment from some worker's hand, and set himself to work upon it, whilst a stream of vituperation pours from his lips. He is usually a haggard and starveling man, himself a victim of inhuman competition. There are weeks when he does not earn a penny for himself. In a good week he may earn 10*l.* The Jews work almost exclusively on men's and youths' coats. They do no cutting, and they seem unable to make "juveniles" and "trouserings."

From the Leylands, which might rather be, from the look of its population, a faubourg of Lodz, in Poland, I travelled to the beautiful village of Adel, some miles from Leeds. At the "Grange" here there lives a philanthropic lady, Miss E. Ford, who has long interested herself in the condition of the luckless tailoresses of Leeds.

My visit was a well-timed one, because it so happened that just then there was being nursed at the "Grange" a young tailoress, Miss Clowes, Secretary of the Girls' Tailor Society, who had broken down in health, after trying for years to maintain her mother, three brothers, and herself on the 15*s.* a week which she was earning. Fifteen

THE SLIPPER-MAKERS 131

shillings a week is the usual wage of a tailoress working full time in a factory, and out of this sum the girl has to spend an average weekly sum of 1s. 3d. on "sewings." The sewings are the thread, cotton, and silk used. These have to be bought in the factory off the employer. The girls have told me that the reels of cotton sold to them at 5d. the bobbin can be bought outside for $2\frac{1}{2}d.$, whilst they have to pay a penny each for machine needles, which can be bought at fourpence the dozen outside.

A girl detected using sewings purchased outside is instantly dismissed. A careful watch is kept on the hands to insure the observance of this regulation; and after the girls have gone home a foreman goes round and examines the cotton on their machines. These sewings are a great charge, for sometimes a girl may have to purchase out of a week's wages several reels of silk, which she may never be able to use again.

Miss Ford told me of a case where, out of a wage of 10s., a girl had had to spend 6s. in this way, and "though the masters would deny this indignantly," she added, "the sewings often amount to 4*s.* a week." A girl whom I interviewed in the office of the Wholesale Clothiers' Operatives Union, told me that she had often spent 10*d.* on sewings out of a weekly earning of 2*s.* 7*d.* She remembered one week when she had only earned a shilling, and had had to pay 8*d.* She had given up tailoring in despair, as she could not make a living at it. She had been in a "punishing-house," and had often been so weak from want of food that she had fainted over her machine. Many of her fellow workers used to beg food off the men in the factory, but she had never cared to do this as it led to things.

The girls have to pay a 1*d.* or 2*d.* a week "for cook," that is to say, for having the food they bring with them warmed up. The tax is compulsory, though many of the girls never use the dining-room, for the reason that the dining-room is often so small that but a small proportion of the girls can be accommodated. I met one girl who had paid 2*d.* a week "for cook" for ten years without ever going into the dining-room.

THE SLIPPER-MAKERS 133

Fines are everywhere inflicted. Miss Ford said about them: "Unfortunately, thanks to the judges' interpretation of the Truck Act, these are legal." She mentioned the case of a girl who had to pay a fine of 2d. when her day's earnings were 1½d. This was for being a minute late. The fines are registered by a timekeeper, who is usually a boy, and who gets a commission on the total amount.

The fines for bad work are very heavy. I spoke to a woman who told me that a week or two previous 2s. had been deducted from her week's earnings of 4s. 2d. for bad work. The bad work in question had afterwards been sold as good work, but the 2s. were never refunded. The wages are further reduced by one-twelfth (1d. in the 1s.) for steam power, and if a girl takes the work home she pays the 1d. in the 1s. all the same. At one punishing-house in Leeds the girls each pay a proportion of the rent of the factory, besides the toll for power. The masters like the wages to be round sums, and odd pennies are confiscated on a promise of a trip for the girls. "But we never get no trip," said my informant.

Subject as it is to all these fines, tolls, and roundings-off, the maximum wage of 15*s.* a week (which can only be earned by the best workers, working full time and even overtime) is generally reduced below 12*s.* In the slack season many girls cannot earn more than 2*s.* a week. I spoke to a machine hand, who told me that for months together she had not earned above 10*d.* a week during the slack season.

Masters take advantage of the girls' want to beat down the prices per piece at this time.

"One time, when we were all very hungry," she said, "the foreman told us there were 400 sailor suits coming up. Would we do them at 3*d.* each? We refused, as the lowest price was 3½*d.* The foreman kept us waiting a day and a half, and at last we were so hungry that we gave in."

"The masters often say," said another woman, "'We have so many hundred articles to be sewn, if you like to do them at such a reduced rate.' We prefer not to

THE SLIPPER-MAKERS 135

be idle, and accept, expecting to have so many to sew. But the masters had lied, and there is very much less to sew than had been promised."

"THE FOREMAN KEPT US WAITING A DAY AND A HALF, AND AT LAST WE WERE SO HUNGRY THAT WE GAVE IN."

The brutality of the foremen is much complained of by the girls. "If he can bully, he is a good foreman." In some houses very foul language is used towards the girls. They are never informed when work is slack. They come to the factory, and have to remain there doing nothing. This is to prevent people knowing that the factory is slack.

A machine girl described her experiences in this respect to me:

"I come in at 8 a.m. If I'm late I'll be fined a 1*d*. or 2*d*. There will be nothing for me to do. Then I'll sit at my machine doing nothing till half-past twelve. Then I'll ask the foreman if I may go home. He'll say, 'No, there's orders coming up after dinner.' Dinner? I probably haven't any, knowing work was slack, and expecting to get home. So I go without it. At half-past one I'll go back to my machine and sit doing nothing. Foreman will say: 'Work hasn't come up yet.' I have to sit at my machine.

" Once I fainted from hunger, and asked to be allowed to go home, but they wouldn't let me, and locked me up in the dining-room. I sat at my machine till three or four. Then the foreman will say, as though he were conferring a favour: 'The orders don't seem to be coming in; you can go home till the morning.' And I go home without having earned a farthing. Sometimes work may come in in the afternoon, and then I will stay on till 6.30, earning wage for the last two or three hours."

TIRED OUT.

The fearful competition in these trades is, no doubt, to a great extent, the cause of the sufferings of these unfortunate workers. Yet this consideration will not render more comfortable, to the man of heart who has seen the tears of the women, and the gaunt despair of the men, the lounge coat and fireside slippers, which have been made to the tears of those and of these the gaunt despair.

IV
The Woolcombers

IV

The Woolcombers

ALTHOUGH some of the Bradford woolcombers frequent "The Swan" in the Manchester Road, the principal house of call of these operatives is the "Malt Shovel," in Nelson Street, a small beerhouse of poor appearance. The one tap-room is roughly furnished with benches and chairs. Over the mantelpiece are nailed two decorative cards, on which are printed, as though in irony, wishes of a merry Christmas and a happy New Year to all.

To the left of the fireplace is a large board, on which each morning the barman chalks the latest tips for forthcoming races, for to the racecourse these workers, like so many thousands of Englishmen, alas! look as their one hope of a little comfort, a span of good time, or, it may be, for the means of escape from the cruel thraldom of their present lives. And even as a woolcomber, the Yorkshireman is a keen sportsman, manifesting all the interest which his despairing nature can compass in our national sports.

As one sits in the " Malt Shovel " one might fancy oneself in the forecastle of an ocean-going steamer, for the whole place throbs and vibrates to the unceasing motion of the machinery which, in the large factories on every side of this public-house, goes night and day and day and night with a grinding and merciless noise, while through the open windows of the workshops there pours forth into the air clouds of foul and yellow dust.

" That soon plays the dickens with a man's lungs," said a woolcomber, who coughed and coughed as, from where he sat, he pointed to this yellow cloud. He was a wan man and pale, an anæmic marionette, stunted and weak, to whom, as to all the woolcombers whom I saw, the word " sweated " could be applied with pre-eminent appositeness.

THE WORLD MILLES GOING HOME FROM WORK IN THE EARLY MORNING.

THE WOOLCOMBERS 145

Indeed, amongst the pale hordes of the slaves of England, no class can, at a first glance, be more easily recognised than the men who are the Nethinim of the great wool industry. Their pallor, their great weariness, stamp them with an appearance almost ethereal or wraithlike. Exhausted by the superhuman efforts of their nightly toil, their movements in their leisure moments are slow and deliberate, a very parody of human dignity.

One is reminded, as one looks at them, of the haschish eater, such langour is theirs. But the eyes, the eyes to which he who scrutinises another man will always look first, have an expression which characterises these men beyond doubt or hesitation. It is an expression of utter hopelessness, of fatigue which surpasses words; it tells of shattered nerves, of depleted veins. It is a terrible look, to be seen on this side of Styx.

It is in this sordid tap-room that the only purple moments of the colourless lives of the Bradford woolcombers are spent. " Low wages are demoralising ; when people get starvation wages, they go to the public-house," said to me Mr. Samuel Shaftoe, skipmaker and Justice of the Peace, the Secretary of the Bradford and District

IN THE WOOLCOMBERS' CLUB.

Woolcombers' Association, to whom I am much indebted. He made me free of the Woolcombers' Club during my stay in Bradford, gave me much information, and afforded me every assistance in his power.

There is, however, little excessive drinking amongst these operatives. For one thing, they have so very little money; for another, they are so weak from constant exhaustion, that a very small quantity of the nameless beer renders them powerless.

I heard of one man " who works at neet," who was so debilitated, that a single pint sent him home to bed, mad. They were talking about him at the " Malt Shovel " on the first morning that I was there. . It appeared that the night before he had had his pint, and, having gone home, had nailed up the door and window of his cottage, so that when his wife returned from work in the evening, she had to break into the house. For her edification, her husband had chalked on the fender : " Clean my Boots."

" It's bed and work for us," explained a woolcomber, " and as for amusement, we get together two or three, and have a pint or two and get boozed." On Sundays there are more pints, few, but effective, and dominoes. When a party gets together the liquor is served in a pot, and only one mug is supplied, which is passed round in good fellowship—an earthenware loving cup—with " Have a soop, lad."

Not very far from the " Malt Shovel " public-house stands an automatic weighing machine, to which, one Saturday morning, I conducted, for the sake of visual evidence, a few of the woolcombers with whom I had been conversing. There were tall men amongst them, but not in one single instance did the machine register a heavier weight than 10st. This was the maximum, and an exceptional case, and there were the makings of a fine fellow about the man who weighed it.

His story was that, having given up woolcombing for tubbing (making wash-tubs for the wool-cleaning rooms), he had gained 21lb. in weight during nine or ten weeks. " I then returned to the works, weighing 10st. 9lb., and in a fortnight my weight was reduced to 10st. It all goes out of you in water. You can wring my shirt in the mornings, aye, and my trousers, too—that is to say, when I work in trousers, for, for the most part, I change these and work in a woman's skirt."

This was an exceptional case, for the man was well built, and at the time had only been working a few weeks in the factories. The average weight of the men fell far below 9st., and in each case was from 2st. to 3st. below what, according to the table on the machine, each should have weighed if in health. One man, who registered 7st. 7lb., told me that when he entered a certain notorious rushing shop seven years before, being then only seventeen years of age, he had weighed 10st. 7lb. The rest had gone in woolcombing.

Another man had weighed 10st. before entering the works, and in a short time had been reduced to 9st. "I then went off to sea for a spell and got back my weight," he said. He had been back a month at woolcombing, and scaled a little over 8st.

But they all agreed, if I wanted to see the champion light-weights of the industry, to grasp fully what woolcombing can do for thinning a man, I ought to recruit my subjects at ———'s works, of all rushing shops in Bradford the worst. Here, with luck, I might even fall in with Mr. Billy Parkin, commonly known as the Walking Skeleton.

But, Billy Parkin apart, any one of these men would do as an object-lesson.

" We calls them ——'s Marionettes " said one ; " because they are that thin and washy and pale," explained another.

" But," said a third, " if you go to ——'s works to meet the men coming out of a morning, you had better take your opera-glasses with you : you'll want them to see some of ——'s men."

And indeed a more ghostly sight than the *sortie* from these works witnessed by me one morning just before dawn it would be hard to conceive. There was so little substance in each emaciated figure as it sidled out wearily through the door into the street, that its sudden disappearance into the night seemed less the result of any movement on its part than of a fading away. Pale, haggard, puny, these men were more like spectres, which the night swallowed up noiselessly. They appeared and vanished, white and silent like clouds, whilst behind them the huge black factory shook and

THE WOOLCOMBERS 151

throbbed to the unceasing grinding of the merciless machines.

THE WALKING SKELETON.

We had halted at the weighing-machine on our way from the "Malt Shovel" in

Nelson Street to the Woolcombers' Club in Albert Buildings, and as we walked on to this, one by one the men tailed off, each to his home. In the end I was left alone with a very old man, Mr. James Berry, who told me that he had not averaged twelve shillings a week all the years he had worked.

"None of them belongs to the club," he explained, when we were left alone; "they are none of them Union men."

He could not explain why this was so, and, indeed, seemed to prefer to talk about "my namesake, the hangsman," and to point out his haunts.

At the club, however, I found Mr. Samuel Shaftoe, who talked to me in the little secretary's office, whilst in the one large room outside, the woolcombers, who were "larking," played at bagatelle or "all fours"; or, inert and huddled up, sat in various attitudes of extreme depression and lassitude round the little stove.

"If the men would only organize properly," he said, "they could rule the trade, which is the most important industry of the district. But the number of

THE WOOLCOMBERS 153

men who refuse to join the Union is a large one."

Yet he works hard to recruit members,

"NOT TWELVE SHILLINGS A WEEK ALL THE YEARS I'VE WORKED."

and every Saturday morning visits the public-houses and enlists as many workers as he can.

The objections to the Union are various. Some men do not care to spend threepence on the weekly subscription. One objection, formulated by an intoxicated man, referred to the action of the club officials in obliging the men, as far as possible, to obey the reasonable demands of their employers, where disobedience would entail dismissal, with consequent expense to the Union.

A stringent regulation in all the factories is that no alcoholic liquor may be introduced into the works. My informant said:

"The shop-steward comes round for the club-money every other Friday, and if a man has smuggled in a pint of beer, he jaws you, though he ain't the —— gaffer, and it ain't no —— business of his."

It is objections of this futile nature which keep many men out of the Woolcombers' Association, the consequent weakness of which is such that, for the present at any rate, Mr. Shaftoe despairs of seeing the workers' many and real grievances redressed. Amongst the worst of these grievances he enumerated lowness of wages, precariousness of employment, unsanitary conditions of

THE WOOLCOMBERS 155

labour, and unfair and tyrannical exactions on the part of the employers.

The particular exaction which, at the time of our conversation, he considered a special grievance, was that of obliging the workers to resume work at noon on Saturday afternoons when there is a press of work.

"Some of the employers," he says, "on the least spur of trade, with a view of beating their neighbours in executing an order expeditiously, to be ready for another, are not satisfied with working these people from sixty-one to sixty-four hours a week, but tell them on their leaving work on the Saturday morning that they will have to resume their occupation at noon and work on to 9.30, 10.30, or 11.30, as the case may be, on the Saturday night. There have been cases where they have been ordered to restart work at 12.15 Sunday midnight and work on to 6 a.m. on Monday morning.

"Now, this statement, on the face of it, would imply that this was a busy industry, but this is not the case. The order finished, the night hands may have to 'play' two or three nights a week, sometimes the whole week, or even a month, or more. I have known firms where this class of hands has not put in a single night for two months, and the first week they have had a start they have been called upon to continue working up to midnight on Saturday night.

"At other times, where there has been an extra spurt of trade, I have known firms to run through under these conditions for weeks together. When the men object to this system of Saturday afternoon labour, they are, in two cases out of three, discharged by the employers. Only quite recently, the hands at one of our Bradford firms objected, as a body, to work on the Saturday afternoon, and did not put in an appearance.

"On this coming to my knowledge, I at once suggested that two of the committee should accompany me as a deputation to interview the head of the firm the first thing on Monday morning. On being introduced to the head of the firm, he abruptly turned round and said: 'I shall not spend my time in discussing the question with you, beyond saying that our hands will have to work when we want them to work; and if they refuse we will get others that will.' The result was that the hands were discharged."

Woolcombing being what is described as unskilled labour, the men are entirely at the mercy of their employers; all the more so that there are always hundreds of men accustomed to the work anxious for employment. A pathetic sight is that of the nondescript and tatterdemalion crowd that each evening gathers towards five o'clock outside the gates of all the factories, waiting for the roll-call.

These are the men who have been " larking " (they pronounce it " layking " in Bradford) with empty stomachs for weeks and months about the streets of the town, and are tired of pastime bought at such a price. They have come, as they come night after night, in the hopes of an odd job. Perhaps one of the regular hands will be a minute or two late, or, it may be, may not come at all, not expecting the machines to run, and then there will be a crust of bread for some one.

As to losing employment by being a minute late, a man told me :

"At my shop, if you are not there to the minute at roll-call, yours is the first name they shout out. Then next night, when you come on, they say, 'Where were you last night? We don't want you. Get out.'

"Then somebody else gets that crust of bread and the ousted one goes 'larking.'"

Another man said:

"If a man is five minutes late at our shop, he's sent right off. Says the gaffer: 'If you don't want to earn your living, go to blazes. There's plenty here as does.'"

And indeed there are.

A prosperous merchant, to whom one evening, at the hotel, I related some of the stories I had heard from the woolcombers, laughed at my words.

"Their stories," he said, "are all lies. They are prosperous enough when you consider that the work is purely unskilled labour. Certainly, the streets which you describe, George Street and Amelia Street, where most of these workers live, are bad enough, but it's not there you ought to see them. It's on Sunday afternoons, enjoying themselves in Horton Park."

"How enjoying themselves?" I asked. "Larking?"

"No, walking about. I tell you, I know the whole business. I was apprenticed to it, and have worked both as a woolsorter and as a woolcomber. Why, woolcombing is so easy a trade that I often went to sleep over my machine."

"And the gaffer didn't say to you: 'Put on thy coat, lad, and hop it'?"

"Certainly not. Then there's all that talk about anthrax, or woolsorter's disease. It's a horrible form of blood-poisoning, no doubt, and people do die of it, I admit; but precautions are taken, fans and so on, to remove the dust, and after all, it is only fallen wool —*i.e.*, fleeces pulled from dead sheep—which is dangerous, and very little of that is used. It's all nonsense, I tell you. Why, some of these dainty fellows even complain of the stench of the wool. I assure you, my dear sir, that I got quite to like it. It's really rather pleasant when you get accustomed to it."

This last statement I repeated that same night to a woolcomber at "The Swan." All he said was: "Come with me," and forthwith conducted me to Illingworth's Corner, as the spot is called. Here he said: "You'll get a taste of the pleasant thing in a minute or two." Just then the wind came down the street. The wind from the moors that blows through Bradford is a pleasant wind, pleasant with the fragrance of heather and other odorous plants, and fresh with the freshness of the sea.

But oh! the horror of it when it comes to you through the woolsorting factories, from the heated rooms in which the wool is scoured of the grease.

"There, isn't that a treat?" asked my companion, and added: "Call that pleasant? why it's fit to knock you down. And that's the stench we have to work in all night long, but," he said, as I hurried away, "if that were all."

The work is most irregular at the largest number of factories. When there is wool to comb, the machines run day and night at the highest pressure; when there is none, thousands of men and women "lark." Sometimes the machines stop for months on end, at other times they are running as long.

This intermittence of employment is of terrible significance to the men, but what renders it particularly hard is that, on principle,. the overlookers of the factories never inform the men when the factories are going to stop. This is done in order to retain the men, to force them to present themselves each evening at roll-call, so that should, by any chance, an order come in, the factory need not stand still for want of hands.

So night after night the men, with their "cans of meat" packed up, will trudge to the factory, sometimes from homes four or five miles distant, heavy-hearted and anxious, to hear what they expected to hear all along, that there is no work for them. And this night after night, perhaps for weeks together.

Each night more gaunt and more haggard, the men turn back from their fruitless errands, to return next day, in fear lest by missing one night they might forfeit their work; for, as has been related, there are always plenty of "spare men knocking about" ready to take their places. So to the walker in the opulent if uniform streets of Bradford these are sights familiar—but no less painful because of their familiarity—hungry men in ragged clothes, "larking" with their backs to the wall and their useless hands in their tattered pockets, who towards the evening set out with some affectation of briskness, east, west, and north and south, but later on come slouching back, with hanging heads, more lamentable than ever, to lark once more.

I have figures before me which prove that the average number of weeks which any woolcomber can hope to work during the year is twenty-five; the rest of the time he is larking at his own expense. One man told me that he had had four full weeks in the past twelvemonths. Once in a previous year the same man had worked seventeen weeks, every night, including Saturdays and Sundays, for one spell.

It is in the winter, when the men would like to be in the factories because of the

THE WOOLCOMBERS 163

warmth, that work is most irregular. The very most they can expect in the winter

IN THE CARDING ROOM.

months is three days' work a week. In the summer, however, when the heat of the workrooms is unbearable, the men are usually working full time; that is to say, five nights, or from sixty-one to sixty-four hours a week, and even overtime, as on Saturday afternoons.

The wages are very low. Even when working full time, a man has difficulty in earning 20s. a week. Mr. Shaftoe puts the average wage for the men at 14s. all the year round. One man who explained "I am lucky and have friends"—for nepotism flourishes here also,—said that his income had never exceeded £30 a year. At the factories where work is assured all the year round, the average wage for the men is 18s. a week.

"He gives you 18s. a week," said one man, referring to ———, of the marionettes, "and shoves you into his oven." And he added: "I wouldn't work for him again if I have to end my days in the grubber (workhouse)."

"It's ———," cried another, "what ought to be in the grubber, aye, and chained down, so that he could never get out."

Yet these wages even are being reduced,

for whilst I was in Bradford I heard of a new factory where 15s. a week was being offered for sixty-four hours of night-work. "Then they don't want no men," was the comment on this news in the Woolcombers' Club. No doubt though, that the fear of the "grubber" would soon fill this factory also. The women are paid less than the men, though, as far as the actual woolcombing is concerned, they can do the same work. Like the men, they are engaged by the hour, and paid by the hour, but they only earn $2\frac{1}{2}d$. an hour instead of $3\frac{3}{4}d$. On the other hand, they only work in the day, and are protected by the Factory Acts, which allow them certain hours for meals. They start work in the morning when the men of the night-shift leave off, and come out just as the men are coming in.

So poor are the wages, that in hundreds of families of woolcombers in Bradford both husband and wife have to work in the factories, the husband at night, the wife by day. No better device for the separation of the sexes could have been invented. The husband comes in as the wife goes out; the wife enters as the husband leaves. It is matrimony on the principle of the barometrical figures.

At a quarter to six any night this may be seen. Outside the factory the men are grouped, expectant, near the door. Now a bell rings, scarce audible above the grinding rattle of the untiring machines. Yet it jerks into life the inert forms of the men, who move in sheep-like precession towards the door, through which, at this moment, a sheep-like procession of jaded women pours forth.

The two streams meet, commingle, and in that moment, and for a moment only, husband and wife may meet. They meet, but must not tarry, for the hungry machine is calling.

A "Hullo, lass!" a "Hullo, lad!" and each passes on his way. Man by man is swallowed up in the yawning portals of the factory, and soon in the long street there is nothing to be seen but the widowed women on their homeward way; weary little dots they seem as they pass out of sight into the dark.

In twelve hours the same may be seen reversed, the fatigue now on the faces of the men, the machines as active as ever, shaking the whole street, so that the foul, yellow dust that pours from the casements dances in the air, at times enveloping these male and female crowds in such a mist that the picture is all blurred, so vague that one cannot discern which tide is flowing, which is on the ebb.

One may imagine the home-life of such husbands and such wives. Yet, as both men and women must work at this trade, as wool must be thrown day and night unceasingly to the tearing teeth of the insatiable machines, it is as well that by the limits of human endurance the two should be separated.

The heat in the woolcombing rooms is at times so extreme that perforce men, and women, too, return to the simplicities of tropical climates.

In each factory the machines are run at top speed; in one factory the employer was able to extort from his machines, iron and flesh, as much work, by greater heat, in sixty hours as he had done previously in sixty-four.

A mere rapid walk through a woolcombing room is to an ordinary man a nerve-shaking and distressing experience. The room is usually about 100ft. long, and in such a room sixty machines, running at full speed, are at work. The noise is deafening—a grinding, screeching noise; the whole place vibrates. The heat is very great, and the air is full of a yellow, noisome dust.

In the daytime there is a woman at each machine, and these are women of every age, from bent old grandams of seventy down to mere children, the rest, for the most part, wearing the *passée* look of middle age. "Girls of twenty look forty," said one to me.

At night it is the men, and when the men are at work, the rush is even more noticeable. Indeed, as one told me, "if they don't see you moving about in the shop, you've got to be moving out of it. There is not much crawling allowed." During the twelve and a half hours of the night shift, two intervals of twenty minutes are allowed for "a smoke of 'bacca in the wash-house," and for the formality of eating. It is eating under difficulties and unappetising. "The men carrying the wool," said a woolcomber, "literally walk

"A SMOKE OF 'BACCA IN THE WASH-HOUSE."

over us, brushing the nasty, dirty wool over our food."

Yet they *will* eat. One often wonders why.

V

The White-Lead Workers of Newcastle

V

The White-Lead Workers of Newcastle

"AND to think that the poor fellows had to drag that!" It was a woman who spoke, and the place where I heard this remark was the deck of the convict ship *Success*, which I visited, on my return from Newcastle, with a desire to compare with the conditions of slavery which I had studied in the English provinces another form of English slavery, reputed even more terrible than that of my free brothers and sisters.

We were looking at a cannon-ball, weighing 72 lbs. avoirdupois, which was added to the leg-irons of refractory convicts. The "poor fellows" thus pitied, included such men as Andrew George Scott, *alias* Captain

Moonlight, "a most notorious scoundrel"; Daniel Morgan, incendiary and murderer; and William Jones, otherwise "Black Bill" —all men of Herculean strength.

Whilst the woman's exclamation of pity was being echoed amongst the bystanders, my thoughts went back like a flash to a scene which I had witnessed in Newcastle only three days before.

I was sitting in one of the women's wards in the Newcastle Workhouse, by the side of a bed in which an old woman, over whom most clement Death had already cast the shadow of his wing, writhed with cries so piteous that I cannot hope ever to forget them, any more than I can hope ever to forget her very pitiful appearance. She was so thin, and her arms were so meagre, there seemed but the shadow of substance in the bedgown that she wore.

She was a little woman, that any one could carry on one arm, as it were a child. One side of her face was paralyzed, and the eye on that side was closed. The face was grey, the hair was grey; the hands, which were twisted and gnarled, were grey.

WHITE-LEAD WORKERS 175

In the intervals of her cries for relief she told me the too sorrowful story of her life.

She was sixty-five years of age, and for close upon fifty years she had worked in

WHITE-BED WOMEN WITH THEIR "MUZZLES" ON.

the white-lead factories of Newcastle-on-Tyne. There was a gold ring on one finger; so she had been married? Yes, and it was because she had been married that she had worked so long and had come to this. There had been the children to rear, and there had been an idle husband to keep.

She had been a white-bed woman, and for all these years her work had been to carry from the tanks in which the white-lead is mixed into a paste with water, to the stoves, or hot chambers in which it is dried, the usual charge that is laid upon the women—that is to say, three dishes of the weight of 24 lbs. each.

"I would carry two dishes on my head," she said, "and one on my arms. I couldn't carry the three on my head, they bowed me so." She was very bent. So this poor little female atom had thus for years carried a weight of 72 lbs., a dead weight, equal to that which such "poor fellows" as Black Bill, Captain Moonlight, and murderer Morgan aforesaid had dragged at times, a rolling ball, in punishment for rebellious devilry. And she had done this year in, year out, as meagre little women and young girls are doing it at this very moment in the free workshops of the great lead industry.

Nor, that I know of, is any one heard to

pity them. Such pity as does go out to them proceeds from the knowledge that their terrible trade exposes them to fardels of suffering, to which the suffering of carrying the heaviest burthens is a fillip of the fingers. To these sufferings we shall come later. For the present we have established how heavy laden, in the literal sense of the word, our sisters are, in the daily task that is theirs.

My visit to the Brighton Hotel at Newcastle—for by this name the workhouse is pleasantly designated—was primarily intended to gain certain information concerning one Elizabeth Ryan, late of 23, Silver Street, a white-bed woman. I had heard of her case by a sheer accident, almost within an hour of my arrival in Newcastle.

A group of women standing outside the "Black Boy" public-house were talking as I passed, and something was said that made me listen. "She screamed horrible," said one, "and tore out her hair in handfuls." "Such nice hair she had too," said another, "poor lamb." I stopped and inquired, and heard the name of Elizabeth Ryan. The coroner's inquest had been held at the workhouse three days before.

I could find no trace of any report of this inquest in any of the local papers, although I searched the files at all the offices, except for two lines in the *Journal*; indeed, as I was informed later by the master of the workhouse, no reporters attended the inquest. The death of a white-lead worker is so trivial a matter that public curiosity concerning it is too small to warrant an able editor to sacrifice any of his space to such an item of news.

And yet, and yet, there may be some to think this death of Elizabeth Ryan, at the hands of an English industry, an event of tremendous importance, not local only, but national, political, universal. She was only nineteen, and she had worked but four months as a white-bed woman. There had come pain almost from the first, but she had remained at her work, till one morning she fell down on the floor of the factory, foaming at the mouth and tearing her hair, "as it might have been in an epileptic fit," said one.

She was carried to the workhouse, and, as a nurse told me, "carried on terrible," in wild delirium. I looked at the entry in the workhouse register: "Elizabeth Ryan —Lead-poisoning." The entry on the following day ran: "Elizabeth Ryan very bad." There was yet another note concerning her on the third day, and that was: "Elizabeth Ryan died to-day." *Et voilà, ce n'est pas plu malin que cela.*

Her body looked like that of a person who had died of strychnine poisoning, and here was a fresh example to illustrate the terrible indictment contained in the paper read some years ago by Professor Thomas Oliver (An Analytical and Clinical Examination of Lead-poisoning in its Acute Manifestations).

"The fact remains," he says, "that every now and then a girl of from eighteen to twenty-three years of age works only a few weeks or months in a lead factory, when symptoms of acute lead-poisoning are noticed —namely, colic, constipation, vomiting, headache, pains in the limbs, and incomplete blindness. In a few days, with or without treatment, she becomes convulsed, and dies in a state of coma, the death being so sudden that we cannot but regard it as due to acute toxæmia."

Again. "For example, a girl works, it may be, only a few weeks or months in a lead factory, when, after having been noticed by her friends to have been rapidly becoming anæmic, she complains of colic, constipation, headache, dimness of vision, and in a few days develops convulsions, or becomes delirious and dies comatose. As the symptoms are so rapidly developed, and as no organic change is found *post-mortem*, the death can only be attributed to toxæmia. Death in these cases is analogous to strychnine poisoning."

Professor Thomas Oliver, to whom our thanks are due for the amount of information supplied for the purposes of this article, most strongly objects to the employment of women in the white-lead works, and entirely approves of the recent decision of the Home Secretary, Sir Matthew White Ridley, who has issued an order that after June of this year, no women shall be employed in white-lead factories.

This order is the outcome of the Commission, of which Doctor Oliver was a member. The Home Secretary has power to deal with dangerous occupations on his own initiative, and without reference to Parliament, and his action in this matter will meet with general approval, if he is able to enforce it. For the order has greatly incensed the employers of labour, who are endeavouring to devise means to oppose the Home Secretary in this matter; and of course the miserable women themselves, seeing no farther than the loss of a trade to which they are accustomed, are greatly distressed at the prospect, and can be relied upon by their employers to agitate against an order which prevents them from sacrificing themselves, for the sake of a miserable wage, to disease, insanity, and death.

Women, as Doctor Oliver points out, are physically far more liable to lead-poisoning than men, and the consequences of lead-poisoning are far worse in their case. For one thing, there are periods when it is impossible for a woman to take the daily bath, which is one of the indispensable precautions; and again, women who are about to become mothers are, by their condition, exposed to the gravest dangers.

For checking a too rapid growth of the population, indeed, nothing better could be devised than the employment of women in the white-lead factories, for the lead woman —according to Doctor Oliver's long experience—almost invariably miscarries, while if the children are born, very few of them live.

"I have known cases," he says, "of women who have had children naturally before going to the lead works, but whilst employed in the works either had nothing but miscarriages or gave birth to still-born children." After they have left the works Lucina has once more been a kindly goddess.

Even when the children are born naturally, they rarely live. I had some conversation with a "bluey" (blue-bed woman), who had had eight children, of which none had lived to be twelve months old. Here it is the virtue of industry on the part of the parents which is visited upon the children. The reason of the employment of women is a mere economic one, for if they are weaker and more liable to disease than the man, they can also be had at a much cheaper wage.

I have collected from various sources evidence which confirms a statement made to me by a prominent Newcastle Trades' Councillor, that " It would take a woman all her time to average 7s. a week, all the year round." True, there are weeks when good wages are earned. The poor old woman, by whose death-bed I sat in the Brighton Hotel, told me, with the shadow of a gleam of satisfaction on her poor face, that there had been weeks in which she had earned as much as twenty-five shillings. The work is, however, intermittent, and, moreover, the power of the workers to perform their tasks is intermittent, for the worker is ill for at least three months out of twelve, and altogether it is no exaggeration to state that for work so deadly, and fraught with risks so terrible, the wage paid to a woman does not exceed one shilling a day.

Miserable as is this wage, and cognisant

as the women of Newcastle are of the dangers which beset them in this trade, they compete fiercely for the occupation. "We have the choice between that and the streets," said one; "and we prefer anything to dishonour." I wished as she spoke that certain French writers of my acquaintance, who profess but scant belief in the high natural honour of woman, could have been present.

She was a very comely girl, and, indeed, of these blue-bed and white-bed women generally it may be said that they are a comely race till the devilish poison ravages, defiles, disfigures. Then of the buxom lass is made a terrible grotesque. Chlorosis kills the bloom of the cheek, paralysis distorts the limbs with " knee-jerk " and " wrist-drop," and attacking the eyes also, may blind where it does not twist them, so that "they get that cock-eyed that they seem to be looking all ways at once."

And I cannot but hold in high esteem and honour a girl ready to sacrifice her beauty, her health, her chances of what is sweetest to womanhood, maternity, for a wage, albeit

pitiful, which will enable her to keep pure and unspotted the white garment of her innocence. Elizabeth Ryan and her sisters may be classed in the very noble army of martyrs.

The lead works are carefully guarded. High walls surround them like prisons, whilst each entrance is watched by yard policemen. The things that are done here are not for the public eye. A stranger could more easily obtain permission to visit the Tsar's palace of Gatschina than a *laissez-passer* for most of the factories in Newcastle where white-lead is made.

"There has been too much writing about us," said a foreman to me. With the Home Secretary's order hanging over their heads, with all the danger to their dividends that it implies, it is easy to understand that the masters should fear the visits of those who may enlist public sympathy for the workers. Still, there are ways to be found into the best guarded places.

Certainly a visit is worth the trouble of effecting it. One first sees the melting of the lead in the smelting furnaces, and a beautiful sight it is, these lakes of silver. Here the blue-bed women are employed, ladling the molten metal into moulds. When the lead is cold, it is carried by the blue-bed women to the stack-house, and each woman carries a load of five stones. They are called blue-bed women because after the molten lead has cooled in the moulds it assumes a bluish hue. The blueys can sometimes earn two shillings a day, and their risk is the lesser one, although there is always a certain amount of poisonous dust in the air. The work, however, at the best is most exhausting.

In the stack-house the lead is stacked in this way. The floor is covered with tan, and on this tan are placed tree-pots containing acetic acid. The "bunches" of blue lead are then laid over these pots and covered over with boards, making a second floor, on which a layer of tan is spread. This process is repeated until the stack-house is completely packed from floor to ceiling. "When the lead is getting stacked up," said a bluey, "the hardest work comes in, for we have to run with five stone of lead to the

WHITE-LEAD WORKERS 189

house, and carry it up a ladder to the top."

Sometimes a girl falls under the weight of

her load from the ceiling of the stack-house to the floor.

The lead thus stacked is left for about thirteen weeks, to be transformed by the action of the vapour rising from the acetic acid into subacetate of lead, and next by the carbonic acid rising from the tan into carbonate of lead, or white lead in its first stage. This is known as the old Dutch process of manufacture, and it is to its general employment in England that the sixteen or seventeen thousand tons of white lead put out annually on Tyneside can compete so favourably in point of quality with that of Continental manufacture.

After a lapse of thirteen weeks the white-bed women are sent to open the stack, or strip the white bed; and it is then, in the cold language of the doctors, that "the first element of danger to health" arises. There is much poisonous dust about, which penetrates through the respirators.

The gaffers, by the way, prefer to call these respirators muzzles. One may often hear a foreman shouting to some girl: "You there, go and get your muzzle on!"

The white lead has now to be washed and ground. The grinding is done by men, who receive from 3s. 4d. to 3s. 8d. a day, or rather double that amount, as, by a curious custom of the trade, two days' pay goes for one day's work. They wear muzzles, but, although the lead is damp, and consequently less dangerous, grinders suffer badly from their employment. Severe colic is a weekly infliction, and the end is usually paralysis.

"The lead gets up under the nails," said a grinder to me, "and works up the joints and twists the arms."

This man, whom I met at the office of the National Amalgamated Union of Labour of the Tyne, was suffering from wrist-drop, a result of lead-poisoning. He could only lift his arms with the hands hanging down, and to raise a glass to his mouth had to press it between the backs of his wrists. He has to eat like an animal, with his mouth to his plate. He is completely helpless at the age of thirty-nine.

"I shall never be able to work again," he said.

He had been working seven years and a

half at white lead, earning 3s. 10d. a day. During this period he frequently suffered from colics, cramp, and severe inflammation of the bowels, and now the power of his hands has gone. Hopes have been held out to him that by following a course of treatment, combined with a liberal diet, he may eventually be able to take some light employment. As he is absolutely destitute, it is to be feared that these hopes will never be realized.

After the lead has been washed and ground, it is collected in large tanks, where it is churned into a paste or dough of a certain consistency by women, who are known as "roller-women," and who work with copper-bladed poles. From these tanks the white-lead, ladled into dishes containing 24 lbs. of lead each, by men, is carried by women to the stoves or hot chambers in which the paste is dried.

"It is after the white-lead has been washed and ground," says Professor Oliver, "and the wet pulp placed in the stoves for a few days, that the principal danger arises. It is the drawing or emptying of the stoves

A CORNER OF A WHITE-LEAD FACTORY.

that tells hardest upon the girls. A few hours in the stoves every week may, if excessive care is not taken, very quickly develop symptoms of saturnine poisoning."

"It is the stove work which is the most dangerous," said one of the girls, "and that kills most of us. When doing this work we have to wear large smocks over our bodies, and handkerchiefs over our heads, to keep the lead from getting to us; but the air is often nearly full of the dust, and gets on to our skins and down our mouths whatever we do."

After the white-lead has remained in the drying chamber for two or three weeks, it is nearly ready for use. The stoves are now drawn by women, who discharge the dishes into casks, where it is pulverised by the packers, who beat the lumps with iron shovels. Whilst this process is going on the air is full of the poisonous dust, and this operation is, perhaps, the deadliest of all.

Professor Oliver's opinion is that the present stove, or drying chamber, should be abolished, and that there should be substituted for it a chamber that could be filled and emptied mechanically. If this were done, he said, and if in addition to this female labour were abolished in this department and the "white beds," we should hear little of white-lead making as a deadly industry.

It is often said that if there are so many victims of this trade, it is because the workers neglect the precautions that are insisted upon by the masters; and it must undoubtedly be admitted that certain owners of factories show interest in the well-being of their work-people. As it is necessary that work should be commenced on a full stomach, many firms provide their hands with breakfast.

The lavatories and baths are in most houses excellently appointed, but if, as is suggested, the work-people shirk the precautionary daily bath on leaving work, the fault would seem to be with the masters, who, in other respects, are well able to inforce their disciplinary regulations.

The fact is, that, in spite of all precautions, the trade is a deadly one, and that if white-lead is to be produced at all, it

WHITE-LEAD WORKERS 197

can only be produced at the cost of human health, sanity, and life. The sufferings it causes are terrible, and these effects of

A SIFTER.

lead-poisoning can never be eliminated from its victim.

Amongst the unfortunate people with whom I conversed in the workhouse was a man, ill in bed, who, although he had abandoned the lead works twenty-five years before, was still suffering from the poison in his system. The percentage of deaths is higher amongst the lead-workers than in any other industry, and not half the deaths directly caused by the poison enter into the official statistics, as the men are dismissed the yards before they are actually moribund.

I have before me on my table, amongst a number of dismal documents, several certificates of death. Here is one taken at hazard: "James Rankin, 49 years, Leadworker, Lead Paralysis, Lead Cachexia." But, indeed, James Rankin and others whose official obituaries are before me, may be considered the lucky ones.

Imagine a life where intermittent periods of all the most painful diseases are inevitable. "Two months on," said a girl to me, "and one month off with sickness is my average." In the end there are paralysis, partial or total blindness, and insanity to be looked forward to by those who stick to their work, because they know no other trade.

The bitterness of the need of the women is most strikingly proved by the efforts they make to continue working—that is to say, wage-earning—when suffering badly from the poison. I visited the consulting-rooms of one of the doctors officially appointed to attend to the workers, and saw on a long bench in a gloomy passage some twenty women waiting to consult him. The keenest anxiety was expressed on their faces; but, from what they said, this anxiety proceeded not from their fears about their health, but from the terror of the prospect of losing their wages, should the doctor refuse to pass them as able to return to the factories.

Such efforts they made to look at ease, in spite of the horrid pains that were gripping them! Yet now and again the pain got the better of their self-control; hands would clutch at the aching spots, or cramp would draw the legs up till the women assumed the most grotesque appearances. One girl came out crying bitterly. She had been told to go to bed, and to stay there under careful treatment for at least a month if she valued her life. She had been earning 12s. a week, and it was all they had to live on at home. What was to become of them if she went to bed for at least a month?

She could hardly walk, yet I foresaw very well what she would do. Refused employment at her old factory, she would offer herself under an assumed name at some other works. The adoption of an *alias* is a common practice amongst these invalids of the lead industry, who wish to continue wage-earning as long as they can see or walk, and is rendered necessary by a precaution taken by the masters, who each week circulate amongst the trade a list of the names of the workers who have been suspended by the doctor's orders. But as the girls say, when one blames them for such imprudence, between quick death by starvation and slow death by poisoning, they prefer the latter.

Each week there is in every yard a medical inspection of all the workers, and here may be witnessed the curious spectacle of inverse malingering—that is to say, of men and women who are really very ill pretending to be well, using every artifice to persuade the doctor that they are in no way affected, and giving way to

A RED-LEAD FURNACE MAN.

manifestations of despair when he roughly convicts them of attempted deception.

For there are certain signs which unmistakably betray lead-poisoning, and the most important and sure of these is the appearance of a blue line on the gums. This blue line, by the way, may be noticed in about 75 per cent. of the lead-workers. It is due, as Professor Oliver has explained, to the action of sulphuretted hydrogen upon lead circulating in the blood, and has been noticed well marked in girls who have only worked one week at the trade.

Of the homes of these unhappy people is it necessary to speak?[1]

That drunkenness should exist amongst the workers is not surprising, for by an old custom of the trade beer is supplied by the masters to the workers as a part of their wages, and the taste is thus developed. Dram-drinking is practised to combat the horrid colics. Under these circumstances, one can easily realize the home of the white-lead worker.

These are the workers whom honest toil degrades physically, most cruelly. When

---

[1] An example: I went to the house of a girl who had died a few days previously of lead-poisoning, and saw her father. He was very drunk. The following conversation ensued:—

I: " You are the father of poor —— ——; are you not, sir? "

He: " How the —— —— do I know. Ask her —— mother."

they laugh it may be seen that their dismantled gums are stained with blue patches. A peculiar cadaverous pallor distinguishes them amongst their fellows. The poison bleaches. I was told of a negro in one of the factories, of whom it was said, "It has nearly turned him white."

My thanks are due to Mr. Dipper, the general secretary of the National Union of Labour, and to Mr. H. A. Innes, of the *Newcastle Leader*, for kind assistance in collecting information, as also to Mr. Jones, who took me to the workhouse.

VI
The Chainmakers of Cradley Heath

VI

The Chainmakers of Cradley Heath

IF the condition of the iron-workers in Cradley Heath is even worse than that of the nailmakers of Bromsgrove, it may at least be said of Cradley Heath, that it makes no pretence to the rustic beauty with which Bromsgrove hides its cruelty as with a mask. It is frankly an industrial town, a town of the Black Country, where, in smoke and soot and mud, men and women earn their bread with the abundant sweat not of their brows alone; a terribly ugly and depressing town, in which, however, contrasts too painful are absent.

One expects to find misery here, whereas in Bromsgrove one looked for smiles.

The main industry of Cradley Heath is

chain-making, and it may be remarked here that this industry has never been so prosperous, at least in respect of the amount of chain produced and the number of workmen employed. It appears that each week there are manufactured in the Cradley Heath district 1000 tons of chain. The chains are of every variety, from the huge 4 in. mooring cables down to No. 16 on the wire gauge, and include rigging-chains, crane-cables, mining-cables, cart and plough traces, curbs, halters, cow-ties, dog-chains, and even handcuff-links.

If chains for slaves are not made here also it is doubtless because there are no slaves in England; or it may be because hunger can bind tighter than any iron links. And chronic hunger is the experience of most of the women-workers in Cradley Heath, as any one can learn who cares to converse with them.

"We has to do with two quartern loaves a day," said one of the woman-blacksmiths to me, "though three such loaves wouldn't be too much for us." This woman had six children to keep and her husband into the

THE CHAINMAKERS 211

bargain, for he had been out of work since Christmas. She was good enough to detail to me her manner of living. A pennyworth of bits of bacon, twopennyworth of meat from the "chep-butcher," and a pennyworth of potatoes, all cooked together, made a dinner for the family of eight.

But such a dinner was very rarely to be obtained; most often she had to beg dripping "off them as belongs to me," as a relish to the insufficient bread. It appeared that she had influential relations, who could spare a cupful of dripping now and again, and who sometimes passed on some "bits" of cast-off clothing. She showed me that she was wearing a pair of men's high-low boots, which had come to her in this way.

She "never sees no milk," and in the matter of milk, her children, even the youngest, had "to do the same as we." These children, like all other children in the Cradley Heath district, had been weaned on to "sop." Sop is a preparation of bread and hot water, flavoured with the drippings of the tea-pot. This *plat* is much esteemed by the children, and the woman said: " If them's got a basin of sop, them's as proud as if them'd got a beefsteak."

In good weeks she could get a bit of margarine, and each week she bought a quarter of a pound of tea at one shilling the pound, and four pounds of sugar at a penny halfpenny. As to eggs, she said : " By gum, I'd like one for my tea ; I haven't had a egg for years."[1] For clothes for her children

---

[1] NOTE.—On returning to Ambleside, where I was then living, I sent this poor woman a basket of eggs. In acknowledgment, a lady resident in Cradley Heath wrote : "Mrs. D —— has asked me if I would write a few lines for her to you, and having done so, I thought I would add a little from myself, as I am sure you will pardon me for writing to you, though you are an entire stranger to me. I have known Mrs. D—— for nearly ten years, and have found her to be a thoroughly honest and would be a respectable woman, as she comes from a respectable family. But what with bad trade she was nearly brought to starvation some time ago. But I felt as if I could not do enough for her. I am very fond of her, as she is a truthful woman, and I try as often as I can to help her. My father, and some more of the citizens of this dilapidated town, got up a Relief Committee, and we started a Bread and Tea Fund for the winter months. You

"IT APPEARED THAT SHE HAD INFLUENTIAL RELATIONS, WHO COULD SPARE A CUPFUL OF DRIPPING NOW AND AGAIN, AND WHO SOMETIMES PASSED ON SOME 'BITS' OF CLOTHING. SHE SHOWED ME THAT SHE WAS WEARING A PAIR OF MEN'S HIGH-LOW BOOTS, WHICH HAD COME TO HER IN THIS WAY."

(*See page* 211.)

and herself, she depended entirely on charity. None of her family had more " nor he stood up in," and when her children's stockings wanted washing, she had to put them to bed, for none of them " had more than one bit to his feet." The washing was usually done on Saturday evenings, when she had finished her work.

This work consisted in making heavy chain at 5s. 4d. the cwt. By working incessantly for about twelve hours a day, she could make about one cwt. and a half in a week. Her hands were badly blistered, and she was

would have stared had you seen her children eating the eggs which you sent; as we say in Scotland, it would do 'sair een guid' to have seen them at their tea." Mrs D——'s message ran—"I beg to thank you for box of eggs, which came to hand quite safely, and which myself and husband and children thoroughly enjoyed. It was quite a treat for us to have such a thing in our house. The young lady who is writing this letter for me knows how hard I have had to work to make an honest living. There is eight of us in the family, and only my second son, a boy of thirteen years of age, getting 4s. a week for blowing in a chainmaker's shop, and myself, who makes chain; and after working hard from 7 a.m. till 9 p.m., from Monday till dinner time on Saturday, and receive 6s."—R. H. S.

burnt in different parts of the body by the flying sparks. In spite of things, she was a well-set, jovial woman, not without a rude beauty, which she explained thus:

"It's not what I gets to eat. It's me having a contented mind, and not letting nothing trouble me."

And she asked me to compare her with a woman who sat next to her, and who was lamentably thin and worn.

"Look at my sister," she said, "who worrits herself." Some money was given to this woman, and she departed joyfully to pay some little debts. "If there's anything over," she said, "I'll get a booster to-night." I learnt that a "booster" was a quartern loaf.[1]

This conversation took place in the "Manchester Arms," which is the house of call of the chainmakers, both male and

[1] At the time when, in the beginning of the winter of last year, the price of bread rose, I felt very anxious for Mrs. D—— and her seven dependents, and wrote to ask how this rise affected her. She answered that prices for chain having slightly improved, she was fortunately able to provide the same amount of bread, *i.e.*, two-thirds of a sufficiency.

female. Beer plays a great part in the lives of the men, and even amongst the women a predilection for drink may be observed. The number of quarts of " threepenny," or even " twopenny," consumed by the men in the chain factories is very great. A master told me that some of his men must have a sponge beneath their belts, as they often consume three shillingsworth of beer a day at threepence the quart.

The beer chiefly drunk in Cradley is a variety known as Burton Returns, that is to say, beer which has been returned to the brewers as undrinkable by customers more fastidious than the chainmakers. A boy is attached to each factory, whose exclusive service is to run out and fetch pints for the men.

The heat of the furnaces is terrible, and the work most exhausting. Men have to wring their clothes when they go home. Under these circumstances it is not surprising that they should drink such quantities ; and as to their preference for alcoholic beverages, a man said to me :

"What strength is there behind six or seven quarts of water?" Some men, he admitted, seemed to manage on "seconds," or milk which had been "hanging about the dairy for some days."

It was somewhat of a surprise to hear that the men could afford to spend three shillings a day on drink when at work, because it is generally understood that chainmaking is of all industries, perhaps, the worse paid, as it is certainly the most exhausting. The master, however, stated that some of his men could make as much as 10*s*. in one day. And this investigation proved to be the case. A skilled worker can make 10*s*. in one day, less the usual charges, but the work is so exhausting that, having worked the number of links needful to earn that sum, he would be so fatigued that he would have "to play" for the next two or three days. Indeed, a man who told me that he could never earn more than 20*s*. in a week, on which he had to keep his wife and six children, added that often when he had completed a week's labour he was so knocked up that he was forced to "mess about" for three or four days.

The work is unhealthy and dangerous. One sees few old men in Cradley. Lung disease carries the men off at an early age.

"The work affects you all over," said a worker to me. "When you've done a good turn, you feel like buried. You gets so cold that you shivers so you can't hold your food. The furnaces burn your insides right out of you, and a man what's got no inside is soon settled off."

This man had burns all over his body. "It's easier," he explained, "to catch a flea than a piece of red hot iron, and the bits of red hot iron are always flying about. Sometimes a bit gets into your boot, and puts you on 'the box' for a week." But the risk of catching cold is most dreaded, for a cold may kill a man. This worker told me of a friend of his who had walked over to Clent Hill one day, got wet, and was dead the next evening. He had also a dismal story to tell of a man who had died of clamming. The doctor had said "his inside had gone from starvation." This was a "middle-handed" chainmaker (a man of middling skill), but he had got too weak to work.

Work in Cradley is done for the most part in factories, or at least in sheds where several work together. One does not see many solitary workers here as in Bromsgrove, and perhaps on this account the wretchedness of the chainmakers is not so immediately apparent, for there is a sense of comfort in gregariousness.

One may come across sheds with five or six women, each working at her anvil; they are all talking above the din of their hammers and the clanking of their chains, or they may be singing a discordant chorus; and at first, the sight of this sociability makes one overlook the misery, which, however, is only too visible, be it in the foul rags and preposterous boots that the women wear, or in their haggard faces and the faces of the wizened infants hanging to their mothers' breasts, as these ply the hammer, or sprawling in the mire on the floor, amidst the showers of fiery sparks.

Here and there in Cradley, it is true, one may come across such scenes as sadden in Bromsgrove: some woman plying her task in a cell-like shed, silent, absorbed,

THE CHAINMAKERS

"A WOMAN PLYING HER TASK IN A CELL-LIKE SHED, SILENT, ABSORBED, AND ALONE."

alone. One such a sight I particularly remember.

In a shed, fitted with forge and anvil, there was a woman at work. From a pole which ran across the room there dangled a tiny swing chair for the baby, so that whilst working her hammers, the mother could rock the child. She was working very hard at spike-making, and she told us that the previous week, her husband and herself had converted into spikes a ton of iron. These they had then packed and conveyed to the warehouse. For this ton of spikes they had received 20*s.*, the remuneration of a week's work by the two of them, and out of these 20*s.* there had to be deducted 3*s.* 8*d.* for "breeze" (fuel). The rent of the house and shop was 3*s.* 8*d.*, and damage to the extent of 1*s.* had been done to the tools. There was consequently left for the housekeeping about 11*s.*

This woman had five children, and she told me that she had been laughed at by her neighbours, because, in spite of her blacksmith work, she had brought each child safely into the world. The work is such that, in Cradley, Lucina is not to these female Vulcans a kindly goddess. One

THE CHAINMAKERS 223

woman, also a blacksmith, had been seven times abandoned by her in her hour of need. It may be remarked that so pressing are the wants of the women, that they will work up to within an hour or two of their confinement.

A woman whom I met at the "Manchester Arms" was good enough to give me some particulars of the birth of "our little Johnny." It appears that this young gentleman was born on November 9th of last year.

"I worked up till five that day," said his mother, "and then I give over because I had my cleaning to do. Our little Johnny was born at a quarter past seven."

This woman made chain-harrows, and could earn 5s. a week at it, for twelve hours a day; as to which work Mr. James Smith, the Secretary of the Chainmakers' Union, said, "It's not women's work at all."

Indeed, no part of this work is work for women, and his manhood is ashamed who sees these poor female beings swinging their heavy hammers or working the treadles of the Oliver. Oliver is here so heavy—sometimes the weight of the hammer exceeds 36lb. —that the rebellious treadle jerks its frail mistress upwards, and a fresh ungainly effort must be hers before she can force it to its work and bring it down. As to Oliver, the name given here also to the heavy hammer which can be worked by a treadle alone, the philologist, remembering the dismantled castle of Dudley hard by, the Roundhead triumphs of the neighbouring Edge Hill, and many another spot in this land, will trace its origin to Cromwell, the heavy-hammer man; Oliver Martel, who crushed kings and castles, princes and prejudice; Oliver the democrat, whose name, by the exquisite irony of things, is now attached to an implement used by slaves most degraded, by starved mothers fighting in sweat and anguish and rags, for the sop of the weazened bairns, who in the shower of fiery sparks grovel in the mire of these shameful workshops.

The impediment of children, to mothers to whom motherhood is here a curse, is nowhere more clearly defined. The wretched woman, forging link by link the heavy chain, of which she must make 1 cwt. before her weekly rent is paid, is at each moment harassed by her sons and daughters. There is one child at the breast, who hampers the swing of the arm; there is another seated on the forge, who must be watched lest the too comfortable blaze at which it warms its little naked feet, prove dangerous, whilst the swarm that cling to her tattered skirt break the instinctive movement of her weary feet.

She cannot absent herself, for as a woman told me, whose child was burned to death in her shed: "the Crowner came down something awful on me for leaving the forge for two minutes to see to summat in the saucepan."

The employing of a nurse to attend to the children seems impossible, according to numerous statements which were made to me. One woman told me that a nurse cost each week 2s. "to do the mother," and 3d. for her pocket "to encourage her like"; and, she added, this expense was not to be borne. She exemplified her statement by giving me an account of the earnings of the previous three days and the expenditure incurred. She had forged 728 heavy links in the three days, and for this had received 2s. 2d. She had paid 7½d. for firing and 1s. for the nurse. Her net earnings for the 36 hours were 6½d. Her eyes reminded me of Leah, and she said:

"We'm working worse nor slaves, and getting nothing to eat into the bargain."

Another woman who was with her told me a halfpennyworth of oatmeal often served as a meal for her whole family. This woman's husband was in a lunatic asylum. "Heat, worry, and drink knocked my old 'un," she said. He had left her with five children, and to feed these (Mr. James Smith assured me of the truth of this statement) she used often to work from three in the morning till eleven at night, and begin again at three in the morning next day.

The work of chainmaking consists in heating the iron rods (a process which involves a number of pulls on the bellows for each link), bending the red-hot piece, cutting in on the hardy, twisting the link, inserting it into the last link of the chain, and welding, or closing it, with repeated blows of the hand hammer and the Oliver worked by a treadle. To earn 3s. a woman must "work in" forty-six rods of iron, each nine feet long, and out of these 3s. she must pay for her gleeds, or fuel. This woman had to make 1 cwt. of iron chain to earn 4s.

The women work on the smaller chains, and consequently use smaller rods of iron. For these less heat is necessary than for the iron worked by the men, who make the huge cables. Consequently for the women's forges the bellows which they work themselves suffices. For the men "blast," supplied by mechanical power, is necessary. This power is supplied either by steam or by hand labour. In either case it is paid for by the men, and these complain bitterly of the rapacity of the masters in extorting for "blast" sums the aggregate of which exceeds its cost. I know of one master in Cradley who employs men at sixty forges. Each forge brings him 3s. a week for blast. The total is £9. His "blast" is supplied by a steam-engine, the fuel for which costs him 30s. a week. He has also to pay 24s. a week to his engineer. His outlay each week is accordingly £2 14s., as against £9 which he receives from his men.

On the other hand this steam-engine drives the guillotine-shears (which cut the thick iron bar into the requisite lengths for the links), the brightening box, in which the chains are polished, and the testing machine, where the strength of the cables is, or more often is not, tested.[1]

In the smaller factories manual labour is employed to work the machines by which the forges are supplied with blast, and here also the master extorts an unjustifiable profit. I remember seeing a woman thus supplying "blast" to four forges. She was a pitiful being, chlorotic, with hair almost

---

[1] Quantities of cables are exported from Cradley with bogus certificates of strength. These cables give way under the strain which they are certified to resist; ships and lives are lost, and the English chainmaking industry becomes discredited abroad. Custom falls off as a natural consequence, and the men have to suffer for the dishonesty of the masters. I have received several letters on this subject. One gentleman writes

THE CHAINMAKERS

white, and a stamp of imbecility—too easily comprehended—on her ravaged and anæmic face. Her work lasted twelve hours a day, and during the whole of this time she had to turn the handle of a wheel which actuated the bellows of four forges. Each worker paid 3s. a week to the master for blast, whilst the anæmic Albino received for her squirrel slavery, "when things were good," the wages of 6s. a week.

from London :—" I am a buyer for one of the large South African Export Houses, and although I was not previously ignorant of many of the facts you state, they came to me with fresh interest, as I have strong reasons for suspecting that a certain firm from whom I have been buying tested chain have been sending me false certificates. I want to get to the bottom of this matter, and it occurred to me that if you would be so kind as to put me into communication with Mr. James Smith he might be able to give me some information. I presume he would be glad to do this in the interests of the class he represents, who ultimately suffer by such practices. Further, if he cared to give me a list of the Cradley and Old Hill firms who are known to be sweaters, I should be pleased to avoid them as far as I could, consistent with the interests of my colonial correspondents." I was sorry, in view of the existing libel laws, not to be able to oblige this correspondent and others who wrote to the same effect.

Elsewhere I saw single bellows worked—at 3*d*. a day to the worker, and 6*d*. to the employer—by very old men and women or by little boys and girls. A particular and

"HER WORK LASTED TWELVE HOURS A DAY, AND DURING THE WHOLE OF THIS TIME SHE HAD TO TURN THE HANDLE OF A WHEEL WHICH ACTUATED THE BELLOWS OF FOUR FORGES."

pitiful sight was that of a sweet little lass—such as Sir John Millais would have liked to paint—dancing on a pair of bellows for 3*d*. a day to supply "blast" to the chain-

"A PARTICULAR AND PITIFUL SIGHT WAS THAT OF A SWEET LITTLE LASS—SUCH AS SIR JOHN MILLAIS WOULD HAVE LIKED TO PAINT—DANCING ON A PAIR OF BELLOWS FOR THREEPENCE A DAY." (*See page* 230.)

maker at the forge, and to put 3*d.* a day into the pocket of her employer. As she danced her golden hair flew out, and the fiery sparks which showered upon her head reminded me of fire-flies seen at night near Florence, dancing over a field of ripe wheat. Indeed this misuser of children is the most reprehensible thing that offends in the Cradley district.

There are here factories where meagre little girls and boys (to whom the youngest Ginx could give points) are put to tasks, during their apprenticeship, against which a man would revolt. I have before me an object and a vision. The object is an indenture of apprenticeship; the vision is a thing seen at Cradley, in the very factory to which the indenture refers. The indenture has been before my lords in commission assembled, and traces of Norman fingers may be recognised in the grime which besmirches this wicked document.

It refers to a girl of fourteen, who is apprenticed by "these presents" to the art and trade of chain-making, at a wage of 2*s.* 6*d.* a week. The girl undertakes during her apprenticeship neither to haunt taverns nor playhouses, nor to squander what

APPRENTICED TO THE ART AND TRADE OF CHAINMAKING.

remains of her wages, after paying for "sufficient meat, drink, medicine, clothing, lodging, and all other necessaries," in "playing at cards or dice tables, or any other unlawful games."

The vision is of such a girl at work in this very factory. She was fourteen by the Factory Act, by paternity she was ten. I never saw such little arms, and her hands were made to cradle dolls. She was making links for chain-harrows, and as she worked the heavy Oliver she sang a song. And I also saw her owner approach with a clenched fist, and heard him say:

" I'll give you some golden hair was hanging down her back! Why don't you get on with your work?"

Next to her was a female wisp who was forging dog-chains, for which, with swivel and ring complete, she received $\frac{3}{4}d.$ (three farthings) apiece. It was the chain which sells currently for eighteenpence. She worked ten hours a day, and could "manage six chains in the day." And from the conversation which I had with her, I do not think that she was at all the girl who would haunt playhouses and taverns, or squander her earnings at dice-tables, cards, or any such unlawful games.

The fogger flourishes in Cradley, no less than in Bromsgrove; with this difference, that in Cradley it is most often a woman who assumes the functions of the sweater. Mr. James Smith introduced me to an elderly lady, who keeps a shed in the neighbourhood of a very foul slum, and employs seven girls. She "has never forged a link of chain in her life, and gets a good living" out of the wretched women whom I saw at the forges on her premises.

Her system is a simple one. For every hundredweight of chain produced she receives 5s. 4d. For every hundredweight she pays 2s. 10d. The Union would admit 4s., for the Union allows 25 per cent. to the fogger. Anything over 25 per cent. is considered sweating. Two of the girls working in this shed were suckling babes and could work but slowly. Those who could work at their best, being unencumbered, could make a hundredweight of chain in two days and a half. Their owner walked serene and grey-haired amongst them, checking conversation, and, at times, abusive. She was but one of a numerous

THREE FARTHINGS APIECE.

"For forging these dog-chains, and attaching the swivels and rings, the girl receives three farthings apiece. They sell for eighteenpence. Working ten hours a day she can manage six chains in the day." (*See page* 235.)

class of human leeches fast to a gangrened sore.

Of Anvil Yard, with its open sewers and filth and shame, one would rather not write, nor of the haggard tatterdermalions who there groaned and jumped. In fact I hardly saw them. The name "Anvil Yard" had set me thinking of some lines of Goethe, in which he deplores the condition of the people — " zwischen dem Ambos und Hammer "—between the anvil and the hammer.

And as these lines went through my head, whilst before my spiritual eyes there passed the pale procession of the White Slaves of England, I could see nothing but sorrow and hunger and grime, rags, foul food, open sores and movements incessant, instinctive yet laborious—an anvil and a hammer ever descending—all vague, and in a mist as yet untinged with red, a spectacle so hideous that I gladly shut it out, wondering, for my part, what in these things is right.

NOTE.—I have to express to Mr. James Smith, the able Secretary of the Chainmakers' Union, my sincere thanks for his assistance during my visit to Cradley Heath.—R. H. S.

Appendix

"I do not hesitate to express the opinion that there is no hope of a large improvement of the condition of the greater part of the human family; if it is true that the increase of knowledge, the winning of a greater dominion over nature, which is its consequence, and the wealth which follows upon that dominion, are to make no difference in the extent and intensity of want, with its concomitant physical and moral degradation amongst the masses of the people, I would hail the advent of some kindly comet which would sweep the whole affair away as a desirable consummation."

PROFESSOR HUXLEY.

CONTENTS

	PAGE
INTRODUCTORY REMARKS	247
THE CHEMICAL WORKERS BEFORE THE CHEMICAL WORKS COMMITTEE OF INQUIRY	250
SOME AMENITIES OF A CHEMICAL WORKER'S LIFE	265
FATAL ACCIDENTS TO CHEMICAL WORKERS	268
LETTER FROM "PACKER" TO "WEEKLY NEWS"	272
LETTER FROM "A VICTIM" TO "WEEKLY NEWS"	274
WIDNES AS A HEALTH RESORT. A LETTER FROM "NATURE"	275
THE CHEMICAL WORKERS AND THE CHURCH PASTORAL-AID SOCIETY	280
THE CHEMICAL WORKERS AND THEIR TAILORS' BILLS	285
A WORD OF EXPLANATION	287
LETTER FROM SPAIN, BY ERNEST REUS	288
"THE TEXTILE MERCURY" AND THE WHITE SLAVES OF LEEDS	289
THE TAILORS OF LEEDS	298
THE BRADFORD WOOLCOMBERS (EIGHT DOCUMENTS)	304
"THE TEXTILE MERCURY" AND THE WOOLCOMBERS	322
THE BRADFORD WOOLCOMBERS AND THEIR WAGES	332
THE WHITE-LEAD WORKERS	336
THE WHITE-LEAD WORKERS AND THE DEPARTMENTAL COMMITTEE'S REPORT	341
THE CHAIN-MAKERS AND NAIL-MAKERS	356
LETTER FROM A GENTLEMAN AT CRADLEY HEATH	362
LETTER FROM AN OXFORD UNDERGRADUATE	368
CONCLUSION	369

A London Editor's View

"I congratulate Mr. Pearson on the whole course and appearance of his eponymous magazine. Mr. Robert Sherard is an uncommonly strong card in Mr. Pearson's hand. I hope sincerely that every man, woman, and child in the kingdom is reading Mr. Sherard's wonderful and painful account of the operatives in certain dangerous trades in this country. What the Home Office Commission has been doing in one way, Mr. Sherard has been doing for us in another. He has got into the very worst of these dens of white slaves, usually behind the backs of their taskmasters, and the eloquent and terrible report which he has brought us from the scenes which he has had the courage and the energy to witness, if they do his pen much honour, are a terrible thorn in the flesh of our British respectability. Just read one of Mr. Sherard's chapters, consider the case of those hopeless and suffering thousands, and then turn to your *D. T.* with Mr. Smugg's, of Clapham, proposal to write, say, on the dome of St. Paul's, that this is the best of all possible worlds. There is something rotten in the state of Denmark. It may be as desperate a task as Hamlet's to set it right, but to have the ugliness of the thing branded in upon us is a first step towards the redress of irremediable wrong, and Mr. Sherard knows how to handle the branding iron. More power to your elbow, Mr. Sherard!"—*The Pelican, August 22nd, 1896.*

A Note from the Provinces

"Mr. R. H. Sherard, in his 'White Slaves of England' series, gives a painful account of the white-lead workers of Newcastle—a description not unrelieved, however, by tales of quiet feminine courage. Mr. Sherard, and the magazine in which he has published his article, are to be complimented on having rendered a signal public service by the revelations contained in this series."
—*Sheffield Independent.*

Introductory Remarks

AS in the following appendix I have frequent occasion to refer to, or to quote from, the Report from the Select Committee of the House of Lords on the Sweating System, I have considered it advisable to print on the first page certain conclusions arrived at by this Committee—leaving my readers to decide whether or not these conclusions are applicable also to the trades which I have described.

174. It is enough to say that we considered our inquiry should embrace—
    I. The means employed to take advantage of the necessities of the poorer and more helpless class of workers.
    II. The conditions under which such workers live.
    III. The causes that have conduced to the state of things disclosed.
    IV. The remedies proposed.

175. Such having been the scope of our inquiry, and ample evidence having been brought before us on every matter comprised within its scope, we are of opinion that, although we cannot assign an exact meaning to "sweating," the evils known by that name are shown in the foregoing pages of the Report to be—
    1. A rate of wages inadequate to the necessities of the workers or disproportionate to the work done.

2. Excessive hours of labour.
3. The insanitary state of the houses in which the work is carried on.
176. These evils can hardly be exaggerated.
The earnings of the lowest classes of workers are barely sufficient to sustain existence.
177. The hours of labour are such as to make the lives of the workers periods of almost ceaseless toil, hard and often unhealthy.
178. The sanitary conditions under which the work is conducted are not only injurious to the health of the persons employed, but are dangerous to the public, especially in the case of the trades concerned in making clothes, as infectious diseases are spread by the sale of garments made in rooms inhabited by persons suffering from small-pox and other diseases.
179. We make the above statements on evidence of the truth of which we are fully satisfied, and we feel bound to express our admiration of the courage with which the sufferers endure their lot, of the absence of any desire to excite pity by exaggeration, and of the almost unbounded charity they display towards each other in endeavouring by gifts of food and other kindnesses to alleviate any distress for the time being greater than their own.

The Committee has, I think, omitted mention of one evil, which strikes one particularly in connection with the tailors and tailoresses and the wool-combers, namely, irregularity of employment, with forced and unremunerated attendance.

I wish to draw particular attention to paragraph 179. It confirms in eloquent language what I have said in this book and in the preface about the lovable natures of these poor people, their Christianity, their admirable

APPENDIX 249

qualities, which should render them so entirely sympathetic to those who have human hearts.

On page lxxxviii, I find under the heading of "Chain- and Nail-Making," a statement made by the Committee, which might refer to all the other trades also. This is paragraph 136, which runs as follows :—

We cannot close this summary without mentioning that in these trades, as in others, we had to contend with the difficulty of a great indisposition on the part of the workpeople to come forward and give evidence. There was no proof of intimidation in any shape that would have enabled us to reach it, but there seemed to be a general feeling that if a witness came to tell the Committee all he knew, it would be the worse for him in his own neighbourhood. The people are not really willing to talk about their hardships or their wrongs. They are afraid of incurring the hostility of their landlords or employers. Feeling themselves to be thoroughly helpless, they dread making enemies of the persons who, as they know from experience, have the power to injure them. The assurance of the protection of the Committee did not always suffice to remove these fears. We cannot blame the workers for their natural reluctance to incur the slightest risk of making their lives harder than they are at present, but we deem it necessary to call the attention of your Lordships to this fact, because it more than once seriously embarrassed us in our investigation.

The Chemical Workers
BEFORE
THE CHEMICAL WORKS COMMITTEE OF INQUIRY.

FROM this report [C. 7235] published in 1893, price 5d., I extract the following :—

ALKALI WORKS.

The Committee visited a large number of works, and made most careful inquiry into the chief departments, viz. :—

(1) *Bleaching Powder Department.*

This department is undoubtedly by far the most trying of all to those employed in chemical works, owing to the exposure to chlorine gas, under the system which generally prevails at present. In the "Weldon" chambers, which are most commonly used, a thick layer of lime, 4 to 6 inches, is spread on the floor. The chambers are then closed, and strong chlorine gas is turned on, which is absorbed by the lime. At the end of about four days the gas is turned off, the free gas in the chamber is either drawn off by an exhaust or absorbed by a lime distributor, and the doors are opened. The men, about two hours afterwards, enter to pack the powder. As soon as the powder is disturbed by the shovel it gives off chlorine gas, and no man could work in the chamber without some form of respirator. The packers, in order to be able to work in the chambers, wear a respirator, commonly called a "muzzle." This consists of about 30 folds of flannel,

APPENDIX

damped and tied tightly over the mouth, with the nostrils free and resting on it. The men are obliged to inhale through the muzzle and exhale by means of the nostrils, otherwise they would be "gassed." The exertion of breathing through the thick folds of flannel shows itself by the red and puffed state of the men's faces, and profuse perspiration on coming out of the chambers, which they are obliged to do at intervals during their work. Some, but by no means all, wear "goggles" to save the eyes from the lime dust. None but strong healthy men could stand the work. Those liable to bronchitis would quickly feel the effects of the gas, which has a tendency to produce bronchial inflammation.

The Committee cannot but express a strong hope that the old process may shortly be abolished for some mechanical process. Meanwhile they have suggested certain special rules to obviate in some degree the escape of gas for the benefit of those working in and around the chambers.

The Committee are bound to add that the packers themselves do not as a rule complain, although some of them have been employed in this occupation for many years, being tempted, no doubt, by the short hours and high rate of pay. But complaints have reached the Committee from those whose work takes them near the chambers; many of these complain of the effects of the chlorine gas on their health.

(2) *Salt Cake (Sulphate of Soda) Department.*

In this department those employed are more or less exposed to the escape of hydrochloric acid gas. Many of the men have had their teeth entirely destroyed by its effects, but this seems attributable to the use of a rag or "bite" between the teeth. The hours of work in this department are long, consisting of two turns of 11 and 13 hours each. The Committee, from their inquiries, are convinced that with increased care a great deal of the escape of gas here might be prevented.

(4) *Caustic Soda Department.*

In this department those employed are not subject to fumes or gas, but danger arises from splashing of the liquor and from the construction of the caustic pots themselves. The Committee have proposed special rules as to the construction of the pots, and the supplying of syringes for treating injuries to the eyes.

(6) *Black Ash Department.*

The danger here is from the unfenced gangways across the vats. The Committee recommend that either the vats be covered or the gangways fenced.

None of these recommendations, as far as I could see or hear, have been attended to. In another place I give an account of the death of a foreman who fell fifty feet from a gangway three feet wide, which was unfenced.

The salt cake men, when I visited the factories, were using the bite as before, never having even heard of the suitable respirators recommended by the benevolent committee.

The lime-millers took a wisp of oakum in their teeth on entering the lime chambers.

The packers, packing by the good old process, had the same kind of muzzles as before the committee sat—thirty folds of damp flannel, which were certainly never moistened with sulphite of soda solution, as suggested in the Medical Report to this committee. Nothing of the sort.

In the appendix to this report are printed minutes of evidence of various witnesses examined by the committee at the North-Western Hotel, Liverpool. Some of the witnesses spoke very

APPENDIX

favourably of the work, others the reverse. I attribute motives to neither class.

Mr. John Beetle, packer, for instance, stated that there was no hardship in packing, that damp flannel muzzles were sufficient protection against Roger, and that the only effect of the gas, when a man did get it, was to make him cough a little. Mr. John Beetle added that he did not drink at his work, that he could do his work twice as well without it, and so on.

The next witness had also an optimistic view of work in the chemical yards, though he himself had lost an eye at the caustic pots, whilst his father had been killed at the same work. I must quote some of the evidence of Mr. Robert Hankinson, employed in the caustic department at Baxters in St. Helens, where he had worked between fifteen and sixteen years. He was examined by Mr. Richmond.

137. Now, I believe that you have had experience of the dangers there yourself?—Yes, sir; I have had a little.
138. You lost an eye there?—Yes, sir, I did.
139. At those works?—Yes.
140. That was from splashing of the caustic?—Yes, sir.
141. Was there any water at hand on that occasion?—Well, there was water down in the fire hole.
142. But no means of getting to use it?—No, no appliances close at hand.
143. But there was a water tap?—Yes, down in the fire hole.
144. (*Mr. Fletcher.*) You could have drawn water there?—Yes, but it was underneath the stage upon which I was working, sir.
145. But you could have filled your water can if you

wanted there?—Of course you could have filled your water can there.

146. But although it was so near, it was not near enough to save your eye?—No, sir.

147. (*Professor Simpson.*) How long would it take to where you got that splashing to get to the water?—If the road was clear it would not take a minute: it was simply jumping from this platform, and then into the fire hole.

148. You say if the road was clear or ready?—The road is not ready at all times, because sometimes the fire hole is filled up with coal, and you have to jump on the coals to get down into the fire hole.

149. But there is a water main tap on the stage there close by that cupboard?—Yes, sir, but it would be handier to get down there.

150. Now, as a matter of fact, when you got the caustic into your eye, did you get at the water?—I got it through some one else as soon as I could.

151. You would not be able to see your way?—I did see my way because there was not any one about me at the time; but I could not depend upon myself jumping down the hole. I groped my way.

152. Then how long from the time you got the caustic in your eye did you get the water applied to it?—It was not very long, sir. I could not justly say what length of time.

153. (*Dr. O'Neil.*) But it was too long for you?—It was too long if I had had it immediately.

154. Was it while you could count 100?—Till I could get to the end of the stage and drop down between the two stages I should say it was a matter of 30 yards.

155. I think the method you have there is getting a man to fill his mouth with water and squirt it into the eye?—Yes, sir, of course; but if there is not too much in, you get him to put his tongue in your eye and lick it out.

APPENDIX 255

156. If there is not much in, but if more?—They wash it then and lick it afterwards.

157. Is that the usual plan?—The plan we use.

158. Have you any such thing there as syringes?—No, sir.

159. Do not you think that syringes close at hand would be better?—They would be better if we could keep them clean.

160. That is to say if they were kept in boxes?—Yes, sir; but they would want to be in a very close box.

161. So as to keep the water in them clean. If they were kept charged with clean water and put in boxes, you think they would be effectual then?—Yes, sir. The great secret is, with caustic in a man's eye, washing it out clean.

162. So that a syringe or spray bottle would be the best appliances you could get for it?—Of course, any one who understands, you know, they get it under a good force of water and wash it out thoroughly. It is rather a tender place is the eye, and any one who gets the caustic in does not like you to meddle with it. They keep the eye shut, and you have almost to force it open.

And lower down:

175. Well, now, in regard to these pots, you have had further experience. I believe your father met with his death at these pots, did he not?—Yes, sir.

176. Can you tell us how that happened?—Yes, sir; I can tell you from his own lips.

177. His ordinary work was on the platform, was it not?—Yes, sir.

178. Tell us what he was doing, and why he was near the pots?—There is a lid that hangs over the pots, and there is a chain attached to it by which it is hoisted up. The lid was lowered, but it was not parallel with the top of the pot, not quite over the pot, and he had his pot full, and he was filling the adjoining

pot; then he was pulling the lid of the pot down. There is a long hook for that purpose, but he had not got hold of the hook, and thought he would not require it, as it was not so far. He was pulling it over with the help of another man, when he happened to say, " That will do," when the other man let go of the thing. and it caused a slack on the chain. The result was that he was thrown over, and he fell over on to the pot, and his arm went into the pot up to the elbow. The result was that mortification set in, and he died through it. I daresay he was standing three feet from the pot at the time.

179. (*Professor Simpson.*) Was his arm burnt?— Yes, sir, right up to the elbow.

180. (*Mr. Richmond.*) Now, what height above his foot was the pot?—About 20 inches, sir.

181. As he fell he must of necessity fall into the pot more or less?—Yes, sir; he got into it, but of course he would not have met with the accident if he had not had his pot so full as he had it.

182. (*Dr. O'Neil.*) You speak from report as to the state of the pot?—Yes, sir. I did not see the pot. I have only my father's words for it.

183. (*Mr. Richmond.*) How long ago did this happen?—Two years ago last April, sir. He was working with me at the time.

184. Had he worked at the pots long?—He had worked at the pots, I should think, for 30 years.

185. (*Professor Simpson.*) Did you ever know any other fatal accident there?—I knew of one where a man fell into the operating pan or agitator. It is like a big boiler with the top of the boiler cut off, where the liquor is run into it and mixed with lime and water, and it is what they call causticised there. He was putting a leg or syphon there, by which they syphon the liquor off. He had a hook or appliances for shifting it down, and was shifting it down when he overbalanced himself and dropped into the lime.

APPENDIX . 257

The remaining witnesses took a less cheerful view of the matter. Mr. James Ryan, labourer about Kurtz's works, working mainly in the open, was examined by Mr. Richmond. I extract from his examination the following questions and answers :—

277. What have you got to tell us about your experience?—Well, I have got gas during that time, so that I was not very well able to come, not in the mornings.

278. How often were you gassed?—I could not tell you exactly, but a good many times, sometimes worse than others.

279. With muriatic acid?—No; chlorine gas.

280. I thought you said you attended the towers?—Yes, sir.

281. Do you work at the chlorine stills?—No, sir, but still I am working amongst both. I have to look after things in the chlorine department. I work on both sides, salt cake and that as well. I look after the pipes.

282. Then were you gassed by chlorine or muriatic gas?—By both.

283. What are you by trade, a plumber?—No, I am a labourer or acid maker.

284. Now, what effects had the gas on you?—It left me very short in the breath. Occasionally I have not been able to get over it for an hour in the morning, first thing after I get up. Up to the top of those towers is 40 feet, and sometimes I would have to rest two or three times before I got to the top.

285. Was the gas that you were affected by in the open or in the shed, or how?—In the shed.

286. You mean that it affected your throat, was it?—It affected my inside, and left me short of wind.

287. (*Professor Simpson.*) Anything else?—I lost a finger.

288. But any other effect of the gas except shortness of breath?—I do not know that there was anything else.

289. (*Mr. Richmond.*) You mean temporarily?—Yes, sir.

290. Have you had your health damaged permanently?—I have not got my health the same that I had when I went there first, not by a long way.

291. What did you lose your finger by?—I got poisoned by red lead, the stuff I used.

292. You had some wound on your finger?—No, it worked under the nail itself, the stuff I used for that job.

293. (*Professor Simpson.*) What took place? Did your finger swell up, or what?—Yes, mortified.

294. How soon after the red lead got under your nail did it mortify?—It might be three or four days afterwards, or it may have been there longer than what I knew.

295. Did the inflammation spread at all?—No; when it started, it broke out under my arm and down in the groin.

309. (*Chairman.*) What were you doing last week when you suffered from the gas?—I have to go on to the top of these towers to regulate the water, and while I would be going up to those places the wind would blow it on to me. It just depends how the wind is.

310. (*Professor Simpson.*) When you are gassed do you suffer from want of breath?—Yes.

311. (*Mr. Richmond.*) You talk about gas floating about in the open, but you are not gassed in the same way as a worker in a bleach-house?—No, I do not go into the chambers like that.

312. What you get is gas in the open chiefly?—Yes, sir; sometimes I don't get much, but sometimes a great deal. It would depend which way the wind would be.

313. (*Chairman.*) Knowing your liability to this, why do not you wear a respirator?—I had got flannel for that purpose, but I might think I would not need it and not bring it with me, and just be caught in it. Besides, it is not very nice. You do not want to wear flannel in your mouth, the teeth tells that.

(*Mr. Richmond.*) Is that state of your teeth from wearing flannel between your teeth?—Yes, sir.

314. That is not a good kind of respirator clearly?—No.

The next witness was William Dooley.

349. (*Mr. Richmond.*) Where do you work, Dooley?—At Kurtz's works.

350. As a burner?—Yes, sir.

351. In the vitriol department?—Yes, sir.

352. Are you subjected to gas of any kind?—Yes, sir, two or three sorts.

353. Where is your special work?—In the burner shed.

354. What is the gas you are subject to?—Sulphur gas; it catches you on the chest and gives you a heavy feeling on the chest. Then you have nitre gas when potting the nitre, and when you have a rag in your mouth it rots your teeth—*I have not a tooth in my head.*

355. Knowing that, why did you wear a rag in your mouth?—A man could not do it without.

356. But a different sort of respirator should be used. I do not see much use of a rag in your mouth?—But where would you put it? If you tie it across your mouth it will slip down unless you tie it tight, and then you cannot breathe at all.

Mr. Richmond: It seems to me that you all condemn a rag in the mouth.

357. (*Mr. Fletcher.*) Do you think it would be of great assistance if you had a better respirator?—I don't know that it would.

358. Would you wear them if you had them?—Yes sir, but you have to get your own, and I cannot afford it.

359. (*Professor Simpson.*) You would wear one if it was given to you?—Yes, sir.

360. How does the gas affect you; you say it is tightness in the chest?—Yes, sir, and you cannot eat anything, and are always dry, and always want some sort of drink to stimulate you and give you wind to last your time out, or else you could not work.

361. Do you mean that you must have drink, and that it must be alcohol?—Yes, sir, to put a false spirit in you.

362. What do you feel wrong with you when you have got this gas?—Sickly, you cannot eat anything.

363. And is that what makes you take whisky?—Yes, sir.

364. How does whisky make you feel better?—It puts a false spirit in you, and gives you a bit of wind, whisky does. It cuts the gas.

365. (*Dr. O' Neil.*) Do all the men in the place drink whisky?—Yes, when they can get it.

366. What do you mean by "cuts the gas"?—It cuts the gas which tightens you.

367. How often are you affected with the gas in this way?—Oh, every shift we are working.

368. And how long do you work a day?—Twelve hours.

382. Are any of the men working, as far as you know, your fellow workers, in the vitriol department, teetotallers?—No, none of our lot.

Mr. G. Burns complained of severe bronchitis.

435. (*Chairman.*) And you think that bronchitis was caused by the gas?—Yes, sir, the doctor told me so, what it was.

APPENDIX 261

436. Do you know anything to prevent the inhalation of the gas?—I wear a big shawl across my mouth.

437. Flannel?—Yes, sir, flannel.

438. Between your teeth?—No, sir, I do not put it between my teeth at all.

439. How are your teeth?—I have scarcely any, they are all out now. I had to get some of them drawn from the gas that I have got.

Mr. Edward Smee was next examined.

513. How do you suffer from this gas?—Tightness on the chest, a feeling that you can hardly get your breath, and you have no wind to follow your work up.

514. How often do you feel this?—There is hardly a day goes over but I get a little or much of it, sometimes worse than others.

515. Anything besides tightness of the chest?—No, I feel nothing else.

516. Any bronchitis?—I feel that in the morning, sir; I cannot breathe in the morning.

Mr. John Plant had worked in the black ash department, but had been forced to leave the chemical works.

548. You used to work the salt cake?—Yes, sir, but by the doctor's advice I left it, thinking I could get rid of the gas, but I did not.

549. (*Mr. Richmond.*) What sort of gas did you get with the black ash?—All sorts: salt cake, burner gas, and others.

550. How has it left you?—It has left me so that I cannot breathe at all except it was a very light job.

551. Is there anything in that black ash department, except the gas, that you object to?—I cannot say that there is anything in the black ash; it was the gas from the other departments.

552. (*Professor Simpson.*) How were you affected?—

Tightness on the chest, and a very hard cough causing me to spit blood. Sometimes when going home I would take a fit of coughing in the street and drop as if I was dead, powerless and senseless.

553. In consequence of the cough?—Yes, sir, from the gas. On one occasion a policeman thought I was drunk, but I had not tasted.

554. And you were obliged to give up your work?—Yes, sir. Very likely if I had had a drop of whisky it would not have had that effect on me, but I had nothing to get it with.

The last witness was Mr. John Mullen, who had worked at salt cake. He had lost all his teeth. His average wages were 30s. a week when working, but he had "known many a week when men have been off three or four days through getting the gas." He could not touch his meat "nights and nights" when working, and remarked that "any man who is not eating his food is not doing justice to himself."

All these witnesses were introduced by Mr. King, the Secretary of the Chemical Workers' Union, now disbanded. He begged the Committee to be allowed to make the following significant statement:—

(*Mr. King.*) I should like to give evidence, sir.

(*Chairman.*) We have your evidence before us, the evidence taken before the Labour Commission: but if you wish to give any further evidence, we shall be happy to hear it.

(*Mr. King.*) Yes, sir, I do, about preventable accidents and the unreliability of the statistics relative to the health of the men. The reason I brought this man Plant to-day was, that he is one of hundreds who have lost their health in chemical yards. They have then been driven out of the chemical yards and sent about their business, and after they have left and turned to something else, and in a year or two have died, and instead of their deaths being attributable to any diseases caused by the chemical works, they are put down as general labourers, and you cannot come to any conclusion with regard to chemical workers in consequence. I could illustrate that in the case of Dick Shone, who gave evidence before the Commission, and looked quite as healthy as these men. At the time he gave evidence I told them privately, and the secretary in particular, that the man would not live two years, and he has since died. Immediately after he came out from the Commission, they banished him out of the works altogether, and he died a bricklayer's labourer. Then I have known men who have lost both arms and legs by accidents which could be very easily prevented.

In this appendix is also quoted an article entitled *British Slaughterhouses*, from a trade journal which is not named. It deals with the packers. Quoted in a book "Presented to both Houses of Parliament by command of Her Majesty," its accuracy cannot be questioned. The writer thus describes the packer in his muzzle:—

The appearance of the face of the muzzled man gives you an impression, which you cannot shake off, that he is being suffocated; the eyes seem distended as they stare out through the goggles; the veins of the forehead are swollen, and the flesh is puffed up in a scarlet ridge round the top of the muzzle.

I ought to have mentioned an additional precaution which is taken before the muzzle is put on. The men grease themselves thoroughly all over their face and neck and wherever the skin is exposed. Round their legs they tie paper closely, and in these gaiters, with their feet encased in thick wooden clogs, they step into the powder. It is like stepping into the flames, for, although they shovel a clear place to stand in, the feet and legs are exposed to tremendous heat.

Their arms, in spite of the grease, frequently bleed. "Let me see," I said to one of the packers, who in a quiet matter-of-fact way was giving me his version : "pull up your sleeve." He hadn't been working for a week, he said, so that the arms were nearly well. They were covered with little half-healed scars, where the corrosive stuff seemed to have burnt in. The packers' arms are in a chronic state of inflammation. To use their own expression, "they are on fire." At night they cannot keep them under the bedclothes.

"*What is it like, being gassed?*" *I asked the man.* "*Like having a hot poker shoved down your throat,*" *was the answer.* "*You feel done for. Whether you lie by for a day or longer, it takes you fully a week to get over it. Sometimes your mate will help you out with your share, and you stay about and make a show of helping, but it is no good. When the stuff has got down your throat, you can't eat anything. If you manage to swallow a bit, you vomit it up again directly. All you can take is drink—whisky is the best thing.*"

Some Amenities of a Chemical Worker's Life

FROM a quantity of newspaper reports illustrating the risks (of every description) to which the unfortunate slaves of the Alkali industry are exposed, I subjoin, *ad exemplum*, the following, taken hap-hazard from my collection.

I
Chemical Trade Depression

"There is no prospect of any improvement in the condition of the chemical trade, and on Thursday, 100 men at the works of Messrs. Brunner, Mond, & Co., Norwich, were discharged. These include joiners, fitters, and labourers in the constructing department. All the shift men have been placed on short time, and are losing on an average one shift of eight hours every week."

II
Accident at Weston

"George Molyneaux, aged 20 years, of Quarry Bank, Weston, was somewhat severely injured whilst following his employment at the Alkali Works on Tuesday night. He was engaged running waggons on to a raised platform, when he slipped and fell to the ground, a distance of about 20 feet, sustaining injury to his side and severe shock to the system. He was conveyed home and attended by Dr. McDougall's assistant."

III
Disquieting Rumours

"There are many rumours in the air with regard to the industrial situation in Widnes. It is said that a large works under the United Alkali Company will shortly be closed temporarily, owing to the accumulation of stocks, for which there appears to be little, if any, demand at present."

IV
Accident

"On Wednesday, Thomas Doyle, 22, West Bank Street, got his hand severely crushed while working on an engine at the Widnes Alkali Works. He was taken to the Accident Hospital, and under the care of Dr. Donnelly he is doing well."

V
Stoppages

"As I indicated last week, a number of men were thrown out of employment at the Runcorn Alkali Works on Saturday, through the stoppage of caustic ash plant. The number of men now employed at this manufactory could almost be counted on the fingers of the hands, and the place presents a vastly different appearance to what it did seven years ago, before the formation of the United Alkali Company. Then constant employment was found for about five hundred hands and all was bustle and activity; now Goldsmith's "deserted village" would not rival its "dead as a door nail" air. At that time an occasional growl was given forth in complaints of the stinking gases emitted from the chimneys and other outlets, but tradesmen and others would welcome revival of the stinks with the consequent return of greater prosperity for working-men."

I repeat that these risks of accident, and this precariousness of employment, should be taken into consideration when the scale of wages is fixed.

Fatal Accidents to Chemical Workers

TERRIBLE accidents occur in the chemical yards. In all industrial enterprises the workers have to face these risks. Indeed, I remember being told by Monsieur Eiffel, the engineer, that on an average three lives are sacrificed to every million francs of outlay. Accidents cannot be prevented, you say. Certainly not. But let these risks, at least, be considered when the scale of wages is drawn up. I give one or two cases of fatal accidents of recent occurrence in the chemical yards. The first I quote from *The Daily Chronicle* of February 20th, 1897 :—

"Mr. Yates held the adjourned inquest at Middlewich, on the body of Richard Griffiths, twenty-five, who met his death at the works of the Cheshire Alkali and Salt Company. Evidence showed that on the morning of the 9th inst. deceased was working near an ammonia liquor vat, when the vessel burst. Griffiths was found under a piece of iron, his head being terribly injured."

The second case is quoted from *The Widnes Weekly News* for August 8th :—

"A shocking accident, resulting in the death

of Mr. Thomas Brady, aged fifty-three, of 20, Frederick Street, Widnes, foreman plumber at Gaskell-Deacon's Works, occurred at those works about two o'clock last Friday afternoon. At the time stated the deceased's son, John Brady, and another plumber named James Bunting, were constructing a tunnel between two vitriol chambers, and a few minutes before the accident occurred the deceased was up there giving some instructions with regard to the job. At the top of the vitriol chambers, 50 ft. above the ground, there is a gangway 2 ft. 9 in. wide, the distance separating the chambers being 3 ft. The deceased was standing on this gangway when he gave some orders to his son, and the latter was proceeding with his work in the tunnel, when he heard a crash, and on looking out found that his father had fallen between the two chambers. In falling he struck against a crossbar, then against a steam-pipe, and alighted on a gangway 21 ft. beneath. He was shockingly injured about the spine, and from the first there was little hope of recovery. He was removed home in the ambulance and attended by Dr. Edwards, who at once wired for Surgeon Larkin, of the Stanley Hospital, Liverpool, to come over. That eminent doctor arrived at 4.20, but his efforts were of no avail, death taking place shortly after his arrival. The deceased had been employed at Gaskell-Deacon's Works over twenty years, and was highly respected both by his employers and his fellow workmen. He was also an ardent worker in the Liberal cause."

I have no comment to make on what precedes,

but will call attention to one statement given in evidence at the inquest, held at Widnes on Tuesday, August 4th, 1896, by Mr. S. Brighouse, County Coroner.

John Brady, of 18, Frederick Street, Widnes, stated, amongst other things, in answer to a question by the jury: "He did not think his father was dizzy. *There was no handrail to the gangway.* There were no marks on the gangway or its supports showing that he had slipped."

I have italicized the passage to which I wish to draw special attention.

On the same date, by the same Coroner, an inquest was held on the body of Michael Carroll. I subjoin the report of this inquest, which appeared in *The Widnes Weekly News*. It is most significant.

"On Tuesday morning, at Widnes Police Court, Mr. T. Brighouse, and a jury of which Mr. Whittaker was foreman, held an inquest on the body of Michael Carroll, aged forty-four, chemical labourer, 35, Moon Street, who died suddenly on Sunday morning.—The Coroner read the police report, which stated that the deceased was employed at Pilkington's works, and returned home from his work about seven o'clock on Saturday evening. He had his supper, consisting of tea, bread and butter, and two eggs, and about half-past ten he went to bed. He did not complain of being ill, but said his arms were tired. He, his wife, and his daughter, aged seven, occupied one bed, and two other children slept in another bed in the same room. About a quarter-past three on Sunday morning the deceased's wife was

APPENDIX 271

awakened by her son Edward, aged nine years, who said his father was breathing very funny. She got up and tried to arouse him, but failed, and then sent for Dr. Smith, assistant to Dr. Allan, who came at 3.45 and pronounced life extinct, but could not form any opinion as to the cause of death. There were no marks of violence on the body and no suspicion of foul play. The Coroner said he would call the evidence, and then if they thought necessary he would have the inquiry adjourned, and if there was sufficient suspicion he would order a *post mortem.*—Mrs. Carroll was then called. She said the police report was correct, and added that about two years ago her husband suffered from typhoid fever and was taken to the Fever Hospital, where he remained seven weeks. Altogether he was ill sixteen weeks. Since then he had not been very well, but she had treated him herself. Four weeks last Thursday he was taken something similar to what he was on Sunday morning, and he had to go to bed. The Coroner said this evidence put a different appearance upon the case.—Edward Carroll, the son, having given evidence, the jury brought in a verdict of Death from natural causes."

I see, by the Registrar's return, that during the quarter ending June 30th, 1896, there were eight deaths by violence, and eleven inquests in the Widnes, Ditton, Bold District.

In conclusion, I wish to make one more quotation. It is a specimen of the critiques to which I have been subjected. The following appeared in the Widnes paper, over the signature

"Packer." This "Packer" insulted me in many letters of over a column in length. I could afford to treat them with contempt, as I held a letter of abject apology from him, for a letter written in his real name to a third party, in which he had exceeded fair comment on my article. His apology came to hand on the morning after a note had appeared in the Liverpool papers to the effect that I intended to take action against certain persons who had impugned my veracity in libellous terms. I learned that he had been for some years a foreman in a chemical yard. After apologizing for the letter written in his own name, he began to attack me anonymously. Here is what this ex-foreman has to say about the terrible accidents to which his former fellow-workers are exposed:—

THE WHITE SLAVES OF ENGLAND
To the Editor of the " Weekly News "

SIR,—Since my last, our esteemed and learned friend, R. H. Sherard, has turned up, and has notified his intention to answer my letter upon the above subject. I do hope that his health has improved by the relaxation from the onerous and important duties he has striven to fulfil. I also hope that his mental powers are quite clear, and that "Richard is himself again." In my last, I overlooked the latter part of Robert's letter: "Alas! How miserable and contemptible does all this petty squabbling appear by the side of the terrible stories concerning two workers, which I read in your issue of Saturday!" This is about the only sensible sentence that has appeared from the pen of R. H. S. Will he please find a remedy for all the accidents that flesh is heir to? If he can, his name is made, and will be handed down to posterity, honoured and beloved.

APPENDIX

But, sir, the squabbling has been caused by Robert himself. Had the statement made by him been correct, or even near the truth, not one would have taken the least notice outside those whose business it is to manufacture chemicals, and the workers themselves, both parties being quite capable to look after their own interests. I am not aware that either the workmen or employers solicited the assistance of Robert, neither am I aware that it was for the public good, or for the laying bare of an underlying injustice perpetrated by the chemical manufacturers. Then for what reason did he sojourn nearly two months, exercising the most despicable espionage upon an honourable class of manufacturers? Well, I have answered these questions beforehand, therefore will not repeat them at present. Yes, sir. Accidents are always terrible when the result is loss of human life; and, thanks to our English sense of justice, whoever is to blame, if found out, has meted out his just punishment. I see, sir, that a sad accident occurred on the 12th at Hyde Park, Sheffield. A young man playing football fell dead on the field. This is not an isolated case on football sport; it is sad. Will Robert put his shoulder to the wheel—no, put his pen to paper—and decry football? If he will, we await results. A young man, twenty-four years of age, was drowned on Friday last whilst bathing. Robert condemns bathing? At Brighton, on the 22nd inst., two men were suffocated by gas—not "roger," Robert. They simply went under an arch to protect themselves from rain, fell asleep, and were found dead. A gas pipe had accidentally broken, hence the gas. Robert! Stop the manufacture of gas forthwith. We have accidents by rail, in mines, on sea, in every class of manufactories, in our sports, in climbing mountains, etc. And chemical works are not excepted. Will this Utopian scribe give us a remedy? That is what we require. We have had more than enough of the "Alas! miserable, contemptible ink-slinging" business.— "PACKER."

A Letter from a Victim

White Slaves of England

To the Editor of the "Weekly News"

Dear Sir,—It is with great reluctance that I take up my pen in answer to the above; but, sir, there is a lot of squabbling, and Mr. Packer is the main cause. I have read Mr. Sherard's magazine article re the above, and I cannot say it is all true. He should have left the drink alone. I would then have held with him; but what I want to point out is this—that if the factory inspectors did as Mr. Sherard, visit the works by the back door, the town of Widnes would be much the better for it. Of course, Mr. Packer, if he is one, which I doubt, knows very little of the working of a bleach plant. He is in bed when some men are nearly smothered at their work. Of course all process men know when the inspectors are coming to the minute (there are certain days) and everything is sweet and clean in a few minutes; but then I don't want to say more than I can possibly help. The reason Mr. Packer has never been pitched up is because the thoughtful people of Widnes will put up with foul gases before they would complain and perhaps drive what bit of trade there is left in the town out; but if Mr. Packer is an ordinary shareholder, I must advise him to say as little as possible— the least said soonest mended. But then Mr. Packer only heard of two men being victims of "roger"; both recovered and one is still living. I am very sorry to say that the boat people at Runcorn did not recover, but perhaps Mr. Packer was away at the time. I maintain that victims of "roger" are a common occurrence. Now, Mr. Editor, in conclusion. I say there is a bit of exaggeration on Mr. Sherard's side, and a lot more on Mr. Packer's side. Hoping you will find room in your most valuable paper,

I remain, yours truly,

A Victim.

Widnes as a Health Resort

MY remarks about the disastrous effects of the lethal gases from the chemical yards seem specially to have aroused the ire of the Widnesians, as also the statements which I quoted from the leading doctors in Widnes and St. Helens as to the dangers to health and life of work in the yards. With that knack for quibbling which has distinguished all my adversaries in this controversy, I have been represented as having said that Widnes and St. Helens are dangerous and unhealthy places to live in, that no Widnesian ever lives to be more than sixty years of age, and so on.

On Tuesday, July 14th, 1896 (as reported in the *Widnes Weekly News*), at a meeting of the Widnes Town Council, other business having been disposed of,—

COUNCILLOR WRIGHT, in proposing the adoption of the minutes, said that notwithstanding that Widnes was such a vile place—they were told it was one of the vilest places in creation, that trees could not live there, that they could not find a vestige of grass within three miles, that there were nothing but squalid alleys, and that no person older than sixty years lived in the town—yet when they looked at the low death-rate it did not appear to be an unhealthy town, and he thought great credit was due to the Council for trying to improve the surroundings of the people, and to do away with the causes of fever. He was sure the people of Widnes looked as healthy as the people anywhere else. The Council had done what they could to improve the sewerage arrangements and the back yards and passages, and if there did happen to be any of the misery and squalor alleged it was not the fault of the Council. Last year the death-rate was 22·9 per 1,000, and for the six months of the present year already gone the rates had been:—15·6, 12·4, 14·9, 12·7, 17·6, and 9·7 per thousand. Considering those things, it was as little as they could do to contradict the statements which were being sent broadcast about the unhealthiness of the town.

COUNCILLOR SMITH seconded the motion, and endorsed the remarks of Councillor Wright. Instead of Widnes being the blackest spot in the country, he thought the time was now arriving, considering the low death-rate, when they might advertise the place as a health resort.

The following cuttings from the Widnes paper illustrate the Widnesian view of the matter. The first is editorial:—

"In the opinion of the cockney journalist Widnes is a terrible place to live in, but the medical officer's monthly reports do not bear out his representations. The death-rate for the past month was exceedingly low, only 9·7 per 1,000 of the estimated population, which is far below the average of the whole country; and that this is

APPENDIX 277

not altogether an isolated instance of a low rate of mortality is seen from the fact that in the previous five months of the present year the rates were 15·6, 12·4, 14·9, 12·7, and 17·6 per 1,000. Many a popular health resort cannot show such results. Councillor Smith facetiously remarked that the town might well be advertised as a health resort. People go to Harrogate, Ilkley, Bath, and other places to drink chemical waters, whereas we in Widnes inhale our chemicals in the atmosphere. This is not always a pleasant process, but, judging from statistics, the effects appear to be beneficial.

* * * *

" While on this topic I might mention that some of the finest peas grown this season have been reared almost within a stone's throw of the Town Hall and the waste banks; and splendid potatoes, sixty to the root, are being grown near Appleton Station."

The second cutting—a letter to the editor—practically confirms what I wrote. I can only repeat that, except at Appleton, I saw no signs of any vegetation whatever.

HEALTH v. BEAUTY

To the Editor of the " Weekly News "

SIR,—I am exceedingly pleased to find, upon constant perusal of your paper, that all facts in connection with the health of this very vile town (?) are contradictory of the extraordinary and worldly-wise Cockney reporter who paid us a complimentary (?) visit the other week; and to have our figures from the Health Committee just as the unpleasant trash appears in print is very opportune, if we wished our friend (?) to profit by his visit. Anyhow, it is not my wish to take up your space and your readers' time by uttering mere commonplace sentences, which can have no practical end. I notice in your last week's issue re reports from the Town Council, that Councillor Smith is reported to have very wittily said, "The time was now arriving when they might advertise the town as a health resort." I wish that might be put to a practical test, as a matter of fact. Facts and figures which prove beyond all uncertainties the state of the town from a health point of view are on our side; but would it not be better, now that our death rate is so low, and now that the amount of gases turned out for our benefit (?) or otherwise is so much less than in former years, to see to the aspect of the town generally, and see if something cannot be done to lessen the wild wilderness look of the place by planting trees and shrubs where they will add to the beauty of our town, and also add to the pleasure of the ratepayers. I take it that the "tub forest" in front of our Town Hall is a trial as to whether the trees will live in the gaseous atmosphere. If that be so, I trust those in charge will give their best attention to the young shrubs and persuade them to live. Mr. Editor, I am a lover of nature as well as nature's God, and would very much like to see our town, enviable for a few things, made more enviable still by the profuse growth of fine trees. Trees of soft wood, I feel sure, would grow. A friend of mine came some twenty miles to see me the other day, and in walking round the town he remarked, "Your town seems to be short of something," when all of a sudden a thought struck him—"I have never seen a tree since I entered the town." "Come along," I said, "and I will take you to Mr. Hodgkinson's farm in Milton road, and you shall see trees in a very healthy condition." We have a healthy lot of trees and flowers at Moorside Terrace, and I believe if the wardens of St.

APPENDIX

Paul's Church, and the trustees of Victoria Road Chapel, would take a few pains and trouble to plant and attend to the training of young trees, they would in a few years be amply rewarded. Who will try? Perhaps some members of our Town Council will try, and then when they get old (much older than sixty years) they may have the pleasure of sitting at ease under the spreading branches of the trees of their own hand planting.

Yours, etc.,
NATURE.

The Chemical Workers and the Church Pastoral-Aid Society.

NONE of my articles has provoked more discussion than the one on the Alkali Workers, which has brought down upon me the strongest abuse from all those financially interested in the maintenance of the present state of things. A clergyman at Widnes writes me that the impression is that I have been grossly misinformed; but most correspondents, anonymous and otherwise, will have it that, with some motive which they do not indicate, I have deliberately and maliciously misrepresented matters. Well, there has recently appeared in *Church and People*, which is the organ of the C.P.A.S., a long article called, "Among the Chemical Workers at Widnes." Nobody, I presume, will charge *Church and People* with malicious and deliberate misrepresentation, yet that its account of the lives of these unhappy people is substantially the same as mine, the following extracts will suffice to show:—

It will interest some of our readers to learn that less than half a century ago, Widnes (Lancashire) was a favourite resort of picnic parties, who flocked from smoky towns to inhale its fresh air, and enjoy a stroll along the well-wooded banks of the Mersey. Now all is changed. The lovely lanes have been transformed into busy streets; the incessant hum of machinery has supplanted the carols of the feathered songsters; tall chimneys meet the gaze instead of stately trees; and for the sweet fragrance of flowers are substituted the odours arising from chemical, soap, and manure works. Vegetation has tendered its silent protest by ceasing to exist, and the railway travellers passing over Runcorn Bridge display their objections by hurriedly drawing up the carriage windows.

And lower down:—

The Trades of the Town

are far from refining to the worker. The alkali labourer works amongst acids like vitriol and hydrochloric, gases like sulphuretted hydrogen; they have to feed furnaces, draw fiery charges from revolvers, pack bleaching-powder while muzzled, goggled and swathed in brown paper and flannel, tend and feed caustic pots, and generally to work amid surroundings full of danger and death. The lot also of the copper smelter and artificial-manure maker is not one calculated to draw out his higher powers. Accidents are very frequent and fatal. We have recently had deaths through men falling off vitriol towers, being gassed by sulphur fumes, or crushed under some heavy load. Many are the acts of heroism to be witnessed in delivering a brother labourer from such a plight. The Widnes artisans are a brotherly, warm-hearted set of men, and quickly respond to any effort for their good.

The town is very poor. Most of the works are in the hands of companies. The old manufacturers who established the place are nearly all dead, or have sold out all their pecuniary interest in the town. It is essentially a creation of nineteenth century competitive industrialism. It is now denuded of the men who made their wealth there; it is increasingly a nonresidential town; managers, clerks and day school teachers live outside, and the town is left to stew in the juice of its own poverty. This is not to be wondered at, but it makes the task of those who seek the amelioration of the town a very severe one. Perhaps nowhere could a better field be found for the Socialist. Here we have a vast mass ready to sink into the quagmire of despair.

Work is very scarce, and many of the men are barely working half-time. Unskilled labour is never highly paid: in sadly too many instances decent clothes, without which the poorest will not attend church, are either not possessed, or are in a chronic state of being pawned. There is compensating advantage in there being this one grade of parishioners. The Church is felt to be pre-eminently

THE CHURCH OF THE POOR,

and it is curious to note how the afflicted of all denominations turn instinctively first to the clergy for help with an almost childlike trust in their power to alleviate distress.

SUNDAY LABOUR

is a great hindrance to the Church's work. All the yards, with a few notable exceptions, have their processes at work in various stages on Sunday; and, of course, this involves numbers of men in heavy labour. Quite lately, what was a twelve hours' shift has been reduced to eight hours; this may be a benefit to the Company, and may employ a larger number of men, but it renders a man liable to be employed more on Sundays than under the old scale. To some extent, it is necessary to keep the plant going; but it may well be questioned whether there is not far more Sunday labour in gas, glass, chemical, and iron-works, than the nature of the processes absolutely demands. One thing is certain: that those who work continuously seven days a week under such exhausting conditions, court premature decay and death. We could give numerous instances of men who sacrifice sleep and rest in order to attend the House of God and the Sunday afternoon Bible Class. One of the greatest

CURSES OF THE TOWN

is drunkenness. Men often have to stand for eight hours at a time in front of a fiery furnace, melting with heat—drawing, shoving, and turning with an iron bar weighing fifty-six pounds. The heat is intense. They must drink. Most fly to beer, in preference to meal and water, cocoa, or tea; and immense quantities of liquid are drunk. The women have no occupation outside their homes, and so have been led into gossiping and drunkenness. Perhaps the depressing surroundings of the town have proved a prolific cause of drunkenness. Alas! the twin vice of gambling has gone hand in hand with it. The Church has had to wage war to the knife against these degrading sins.

This is strong confirmation of what I wrote. Further proof is afforded in the preceding pages.

As to this article on "The Alkali Workers," I must say that, if it has brought me in for much abuse, it has also excited widespread indignation of another kind : that is to say, in sympathy with me. It has been translated—to my knowledge— into French,[1] German, Italian, Spanish, and Nor-

[1] See *Le Petit Parisien*, inter alia, for August 29th, 1896, in leading article : "On a frémi," writes Jean Frollo, "à ces révélations, même parmi les faiseurs d'affaires de Londres, qui ne se piquent pas d'une grande sentimentalité. Elles ont inspiré une émotion dont nous avons l'écho." And further down : "La divulgation de ces faits a produit, comme je l'ai dit, une grande impression de

wegian,[2] and was largely quoted in the Japanese newspapers, the alkali industry being one in which Japan is greatly interested.

pitié. Mais après ce mouvement d'indignation, n'est-il pas à craindre que les choses aillent comme auparavant?"

[2] I have reasons to hope that the quotations from this article in the Norwegian papers will prevent the establishment of chemical yards in that country, as recently promised by certain capitalists.

The Chemical Workers and their Tailors' Bills

THE following, taken from the article on *British Slaughter Houses* which is printed in the report to the Home Secretary, fully confirms what I have said about the effect of the gas, etc., on the men's clothes :—

"The man who lent me his muzzle was in his working togs, wooden clogs, paper leggings over his trousers. I got him to give me his clothes' bill for a fortnight. The items are as follows. They were checked by a number of other men, and are under rather than over the mark :—

	s.	d.
"5 cotton shirts at 1s. 2d.	5	10
1 pair of clogs in three weeks at 3s. 6d.	2	4
1 singlet at 3s.	3	0
1 pair trousers, with patchings, at 3s.	3	0
Flannel for renewing muzzle	1	0
	15	2

"These particulars were somewhat staggering, but the packer asked me to look at his clothes. His shirt was torn, I noticed, and in several parts hung in strips. It was hardened by the acid or powder, and tore freely wherever one laid hold of it. This shirt had seen two days' work, and was now good for nothing. Through the rents the chlorine gets at the flannel singlet and attacks that. His trousers were held together by some rough patches. Patching clothes is, however, out of the question as a rule. I tried to get a pin through the shirt, but the stuff was so caked and stiffened with the sweat and powder that it was like pushing it through plaster. 'Besides,' said the men, 'we can't ask our wives to patch our clothes. The acid gets at the ends of their fingers and burns them. There is nothing for it but to be continually buying fresh things as the old ones give out.'"

A WORD OF EXPLANATION

IT is necessary for me to state that my article on the Alkali Workers in no way refers to the employees either of Brunner, Mond & Co., or of the Messrs. Lever, of Sunlight Soap, who manufacture their own chemicals. I was informed on every side that both these firms treat their men with fairness and even liberality. The Messrs. Lever, in particular, enjoy the reputation throughout Cheshire and Lancashire of being model employers, and Port Sunlight is spoken of in the slums of Widnes as the El Dorado of the chemical worker's ambition, where men in health can save money, can come to possess their own cottages, and make provision for their old age, and in sickness receive careful attention and humane treatment. The same, I believe, may be said of the Brunner Mond Works. It is fair to mention this.

R. H. SHERARD.

Letter from Spain

Press Libels on Industry

(To the Editor of *The Textile Mercury*)

Sir, I receive your journal regularly, and apart from a business point of view always read with interest your articles inspired by patriotic sentiments. I refer particularly to your denunciation of those scandalous articles in *Pearson's Magazine*. Your remark that they would be repeated in American papers is doubtless quite correct. To-day, picking up an insignificant Spanish paper, I find a translation of another article, perhaps even more scandalous, on "The Chemical Trades in St. Helens." English journalism has hitherto stood so high in Continental opinion that anything published passes as gospel truth. The difficulty is, it is almost impossible to stop these mischievous libels. Still there is one way—I make it as a suggestion—and wonder that it has not occurred before. It is impossible by law to get at the root of mischievous journalism, but why should not the Press apply for incorporation and form a body like lawyers, doctors, dentists, etc.? A committee of the board could then deal with such things as libel, dickturpinism, and scurrilous literature. They could take powers to this end. You will grasp my meaning and perhaps work out the idea.

Yours, etc
ERNEST REUS.

Barcelona.

"The Textile Mercury" and The White Slaves of Leeds

THE leading organ of the textile industry—it claims to have "the largest textile circulation in the world," whatever a "textile circulation" may be—is a trade paper, published in Manchester, called *The Textile Mercury*, with which—mark it—is incorporated *The Hosiery and Lace Trades' Review*. This organ depends on employers for its circulation and on manufacturers of the commodities needed by these employers for its advertisements. It is not, therefore, surprising that it should have taken up arms against me for my statements about the abominable sweating which is going on in certain branches of the textile industries. It is, on the contrary, a matter for surprise that its excessive fervour on behalf of the people from whom it draws its sustenance should have led it to commit itself to a series of very gross libels upon me. I am charged by the editor of *The Textile Mercury* with falsehood, slander, and "traduction." I presume traducement was meant. I really thought that Manchester people were more level-headed and prudent than this.

The first article of the "White Slaves" series which was dealt with by *The Textile Mercury* was the one on "The Slipper Makers and Tailors of Leeds." In the issue of that periodical for September 5th there appeared two leading articles. The first is headed "LIBELS ON THE NATION." It opens with an attack on the American newspapers and professional politicians, "whose object has been to bolster up a fictitious case for high protection on the basis of inaccurate statements regarding the alleged pauper labour of Europe, with special reference to that of England," and continues in the following words:—

"We were not, however, prepared to believe in the possibility of English journals joining in the lying and libellous attacks which have been made upon our industrial life generally by some American papers until we saw the current issue of *Pearson's Monthly*, published on Tuesday. That smartly conducted publication contains an article (one of a series on 'The White Slaves of England') entitled 'The Slipper Makers and Tailors of Leeds,' which is so full of misrepresentations that it is absolutely unfair to the readers of the magazine to allow them to go undisputed. It is a curious coincidence that a member of *The Textile Mercury* staff happened to call upon a Leeds firm a short time after it had been visited by a gentleman representing *Pearson's*, and, from the facts gleaned, it appears that a request was made for material to form a portion of the series of articles on 'Gates and Pillars of the Empire,' now running in the magazine referred to. It will be observed that there was no reference to the series on 'The White Slaves of England,' to mention which, when approaching a high-class house, would have been to arouse suspicions as to the *bond fides* of the whole thing. But the subsequent publication of the August number of *Pearson's* did arouse the suspicion on the part of the gentlemen referred to that one of the tricks of the new journalism was being attempted; and the publication of the September *Pearson's* fully confirmed this belief, for in it an attempt has been made to paint the condition of the Leeds tailors as that of 'White Slaves.' When a journalist receives instructions from his editor to execute a certain commission, it is his duty to obey to the best of his ability; but in selecting Leeds as the gathering ground for such facts as were sought in this particular instance a very serious mistake was made; for the Leeds tailors, applying that term to the operatives connected with the ready-made clothing trade of the town, are not only well paid as a body, but present at their work a very cheerful appearance."

I may say at once that I have not the faintest idea to what "trick of the new journalism" the member of *The Textile Mercury* staff refers. Mr. Robert Machray, of *Pearson's Magazine*, visited Leeds for the purpose of his admirable articles on "Gates and Pillars of the Empire," but I knew nothing about it until the article appeared, nor have I the honour of being acquainted with Mr. Machray. I mention this as illustrating the perspicacity and accuracy of the *Mercury's* commissioner. The leading article continues as follows:—

" The writer of the ' White Slaves ' article is

careful to modify his reference to the tailoring trade by the admission that, 'in comparison to the slipper-makers, the tailors and tailoresses of Leeds have a prosperous time.' References are made to the 'abominable quality of much of the cloth which is given them to work into clothes,' and we find one cutter speaking of quantities of string, cork, feathers, wire, and stones, found in certain cloths, and stating that when the circular, steam-driven knife—with which thirty or forty double thicknesses of cloth are cut out, according to the pattern chalked on the top piece—comes into contact either with stone or wire, 'the danger of its breaking is very great.' So would the danger be great if the knife came into contact with a railway arch or a suspension bridge, which, luckily, are no more the components of English cloth than stones."

This is mere negation of fact. The cutter in question afforded me proof *de visu* of the accuracy of his statements. The cheapest cloth used in the Leeds tailoring trade does contain the foreign non-textile components referred to, as any one who cares to test it can see for himself. I confess that, at first, I was inclined to disbelieve his assertion that this cloth was sized with pig's manure, but, as I relate in my article, this was confirmed by a Yorkshire squire, whom I met at the North-Eastern Hotel in Newcastle.

The conclusion of the article is characteristic. These be the bowels of compassion of gentlemen who derive their sustenance from the employers of the white slaves:—

"As an illustration of the bias with which the

article is throughout heavily tinged, the following extract is given:

"'In the one downstairs room of a house in one of the lowest neighbourhoods in Leeds, I found an old slipper-maker at his tea. Although it was then past ten at night, his five little children were up and with him. As his wife explained, "They've got to be there when there's something to eat going. Father chucks them a bit of bread now and again, and so they likes to be there."'

"'They likes to be there'! Of course they do. There are scores of thousands of well-fed and happy children in England who 'likes to be there' when 'dad' is having his meals. If the writer of the paragraph quoted means to insinuate that the children referred to live on scraps of bread thrown from their father's table, why does he not say so openly? And if he cannot substantiate his assertion, what does he mean by writing such nonsense?"

I thought that I had told the pitiful story in the plainest terms. But none so blind as those who won't see. *Le grand art de ne pas tout dire* is a literary axiom which is apparently unknown in the Manchester trade press. These wretched, half-naked, half-famished babes were out of bed —if bed there was—to get what food fell from the father's table. It was one of the saddest sights that I have ever seen. Two other men were present and saw and heard what I have told. We were all glad to get away into the noisome slum without.

The second article is entitled, "THE TAILORING

TRADE OF LEEDS." From subsequent references to it in *The Textile Mercury*, I gather that it purports to be a refutation, or rather "an exposure of the inaccuracies" in my article on the conditions under which the tailors and tailoresses of Leeds have to work. It refutes nothing. I stated that the men complain of little except the filthy nature of some of the cloth on which they have to work. My article chiefly deals with the miserable condition of many of the unfortunate Jews in the Leylands' sweating-dens, and of the tailoresses in the "punishing-houses." As to the latter, I cited a witness whose evidence even *The Textile Mercury* must admit to be unimpeachable, Miss E. Ford, of Adel Grange, a wealthy lady, who for years has worked on behalf of these unhappy girls. It was at her house that I met and interviewed Miss Clowes, under the circumstances described. *The Textile Mercury* passes all their statements over in silence. There is not a word about "fines," or "cook," or "sewings," or forced attendance when no work is supplied, or any of the other grievances of which the girls complain. The article opens with a description of the factory where *The Textile Mercury's* representative followed the innocent and unsuspecting Mr. Robert Machray.

"The Tailoring Trade of Leeds

" The writer of the articles on alleged 'White Slavery in England' does not appear to be satisfied with the truth if it does not answer his purpose. This fact has been pointedly brought home to us from the circumstance that

APPENDIX 295

in the factory where *The Textile Mercury's* representative trod so closely on his heels he saw nothing to furnish him with the special material required, and therefore wisely refrains from mentioning the matter. We will supply the deficiency by stating that there are over 1,100 hands employed in the factory, three-fourths being females. There are no half-timers in the trade, and, in fact, no hands are employed below fourteen. The average earnings for this very large number of operatives, inclusive of the younger hands, who form a large proportion of the total, are 15s. a week. There are many getting 20s. and a large number earning 25s. In some cases, where there is exceptional skill and experience, the earnings amount to an average of 30s. These facts are derived from the wage books of two firms employing between them about 4,000 hands. They are firms whose premises, from basement to ceiling, are constructed on the most sanitary principles, and the greatest cleanliness prevails throughout, while the workers are exceptionally cleanly and cheerful in appearance. They are not exceptional firms, but only two out of many where the conditions of labour are of the pleasantest."

What have I to do with Hecuba, and what has Hecuba to do with me?

My description of the sweating-dens in the Leylands is characterized in the following words:—

" Here is a picture intended as a representation of the great clothing trade of Leeds, which, if true, would be a disgrace to the nation. But it is fortunately a grossly incorrect drawing, and one which reflects discredit both on the writer and any journal which would publish it, knowing it to be false, which *Pearson's*, of course, did not. The bulk of the Leeds clothing trade is conducted in roomy factories of the best architectural and sanitary type, and the insinuation that a Leeds ready-made garment has probably been lying on a floor in 'the filth and the vermin,' is a slander of the basest kind upon such houses as John Barran & Sons, Arthur & Co., Ltd., Stewart & Macdonald, Mann, Byars & Co., J. and W. Campbell & Co., Hunter, Barr, & Co., and many other fine firms in Leeds, which form the backbone of its great clothing trade."

So because Messrs. Poole, and Doré, and Samuelson, and the Bond Street and Vigo Street tailors treat their employés fairly, there is no sweating in the tailoring trade in London.

The article concludes as follows:

"The spirit of misrepresentation which permeates the whole article receives a further illustration in the following extract:—

"'Masters take advantage of the girls' want to beat down the prices per piece at this time. "One time, when we were all very hungry," she said, "the foreman told us there were 400 sailor suits coming up. Would we do them at 3d. each? We refused, as the lowest price was 3½d. The foreman kept us waiting a day and a half, and at last we were so hungry that we gave in."'

"We have here a suggestion that sailors' suits are actually made for 3d. each. As a matter of fact

APPENDIX

work in the clothing trade is so sub-divided that a pair of trousers will pass through as many as ten hands before being ready for the stock room, while some garments pass through even a larger number. One portion of the work will be taken up by girls who simply make button-holes (by machinery), while others baste, seam, braid, and so on. And yet in the face of such facts the writer in *Pearson's* deliberately suggests that suits have been made for 3d. each, leaving the general reader to suppose not only that the work of making a garment is carried out by one pair of hands from beginning to end, but that Leeds is a sweating den which would disgrace even Germany. It is to be hoped that these base calumnies will not be allowed to pass unnoticed in Leeds itself."

"The writer in *Pearson's*" deliberately suggested nothing. He reported in her own words the statement of a machine girl, a statement which was made in the presence of four witnesses. These were ladies and gentlemen—the interview took place in the drawing-room of a private house—who were interested in this girl, and who attested to her absolute reliability.

I may add, in conclusion, that the above article in *The Textile Mercury* is the only refutation or exposure of my inaccuracies which has appeared anywhere. It is for the reader to decide what it is worth. In despite of the editor's hopes, the Leeds newspapers let my "calumnies" pass.

The Tailors of Leeds

EXTRACTS from Copy of Report to the Board of Trade on THE SWEATING SYSTEM in Leeds (by the Labour Correspondent of the Board). Presented to both Houses of Parliament by command of Her Majesty.

This Report (C—5513) is dated June 13th, 1888, and deals chiefly with the Jewish tailors. Since 1888 matters have not improved, for competition has greatly increased. In 1888 there were not more than 7,000 Jews in Leeds.

I extract the following paragraphs from this Report :—

There were present at the meeting (a meeting convened for the purpose by Miss Potter) where these statements were made, eight employers, who found work for 400 workpeople. They somewhat differed as to the regularity of employment: one stating his average at four days per week, another at three and a half, others at five and five and a half days, while some were not inclined to answer the question.

The men, on the other hand, stated that "their average amount of work per week" was "three days, though in some cases it will run to three and a half days, but in others it is not more than two days."

The day consisted of twelve hours. Sixty-two hours was a week's work.

Employers and men differed as to wages paid.

APPENDIX 299

The following table shows the divergence of their statements.

STATEMENTS OF MASTERS AND WORKMEN AS TO WAGE RATES PAID IN LEEDS TAILORS' SHOPS UNDER THE SWEATING SYSTEM.

Branch of Trade.	Masters' Statement.	Men's Statement.
Fixers	6s. to 7s. 6d.	6s. to 6s. 2d.
Machinists (Male). . . .	6s. to 7s. 6d.	6s. to 6s. 8d.
„ „ inferior	2s. 6d. to 5s.	2s. to 5s. 6d.
„ (Female) . . .	5s. to 6s.	5s. to 5s. 2d.
„ „ inferior	—	10d. to 3s. 6d.
Pressers off	5s. 6d. to 7s.	4s. to 6s.
„ under	1s. 8d. to 4s.	10d. to 2s. 8d.
Fellers (Female)	2s. to 3s.	1s. 9d. to 2s. 3d.
Button-sewers-on	2s. to 3s.	—
Basters (out).	8s. to 5s.	2s. 6d. to 4s.
„ (under).	4s. 6d. to 6s. 6d.	4s. 8d. to 5s. 6d.
Button-holers	4s. to 5s.	—

Extracts from the Fifth Report, from the Select Committee of the House of Lords on the Sweating System (ordered to be printed 28th April, 1890).

50. Mr. Rickards, the Inspector for the Leeds District, under the Factory and Workshop Act, stated that he had over 2,000 factories and about 3,000 workshops subject to his jurisdiction. The district extends over a considerable area, and there is but one assistant. The clothing trade in Leeds, as all the evidence bearing upon it had led us to anticipate, has developed greatly, according to Mr. Rickards, especially within the last twenty years. The number of foreigners employed in the business has also largely increased.

Rickards, 3090.

3909–13.	There are now ninety-seven Jewish workshops in the city, whereas five years ago there were scarcely a dozen. The number of Jews engaged in the tailoring trade is about three thousand.
Cohen, 30525.	The whole Jewish population of Leeds is about five thousand, according to the estimate of the treasurer of the Jewish Board of Guardians. The same process goes on here as in London and other cities. The immigrants arrive with very scanty means, or none, and without a knowledge
Rickards, 30823–4.	of any trade. They go to their friends or to the Jewish Board of Guardians for assistance, and take to tailoring because it is easily learnt, and employment in it is soon found. They soon find themselves able to earn a moderate living. There can be no doubt that they also soon begin to entice their friends and fellow-countrymen over here, and thus the supply of labour is constantly
3)017–20; 3.	kept up. But, according to Mr. Rickards, in Leeds it does not exceed the demand, so great is the present extension of the clothing trade.
30942.	51. Speaking of the Jewish shops, and especially with respect to closet accommodation, Mr. Rickards described their sanitary condition as
30343.	"simply appalling" down to 1888. No one had ever complained to him; he had "no notion that anything of the kind existed to such an extent." Some improvement, however, had taken place since that time, and the shops themselves were generally fairly clean. Mr. Newhouse, the chief
Newhouse, 30126.	Sanitary Inspector, stated that they had prohibited a great number of dwellings from taking in lodgers, and had entirely closed a large number of dwellings as unfit for habitation. Speaking of the Jewish workshops, he said he found some of them last year "in an insanitary condition; the
30111.	walls and floors dirty, a want of ventilation, and insufficient closet accommodation." Generally

speaking, the sanitary condition was "fairly good."

52. The statements made by the workpeople varied on some material points, but their general effect may be briefly summarised. One of the women stated that she earned from 14s. to 16s. a week, and even as a beginner had never received less than 3s. a week. But she had some experience of sewing before going to the workshop, so that she was not a raw hand. A "presser" earned from 4s. 6d. to 5s. a day. His hours were from eight till eight, or sometimes till nine. Sometimes he had worked up till two or three in the morning. For three or four months in the year he is out of work. Four days' work a week is about as much as he is able to get. Another "greener," a German, explained that he had come over to England without any means, and that he had given a man "half a quid" (10s.) to teach him the use of the sewing machine. Besides giving the 10s., he worked four weeks for nothing, and then went to another shop, where he worked for 6s. a week for nearly a year. Then he "got to be a plain machinist," and received 2s. a day, rising in time to 4s. The system has been fully described in previous sections of this Report, and it follows the usual course at Leeds.

53. Mr. Sweeney, who, though neither a Jew nor a tailor, is Secretary to the Jewish Tailors' Trade Society, stated that most of the sweaters or middlemen were Jews, and that the majority of them had no practical knowledge of their trade. They obtain work, he stated, by bribing managers. He also complained that the sweaters ill-treated their hands, and drove them too hard. A member of the firm of J. W. Denton & Co. admitted that the charge of bribery had often

been made, but he had never succeeded in finding out a case. It may well be, however, that the head of a firm, or one of the managers, is not in the best possible position to ascertain the truth on such a subject. A different light was thrown upon the question by the evidence of Mr. Lubelski, now a wholesale clothing manufacturer, who was formerly a journeyman tailor. He stated that bribery was practised, and that he had been obliged to resort to it himself. "If I happened to miss giving any bribery, I suddenly was stopped of a bit of work." The middleman, being compelled to bribe the foreman, cuts down the wages of the workers to recoup himself. Mr. David Isaac also gave some valuable evidence on this point. He is not personally interested in the clothing trade, and may, therefore, be considered to take an impartial view of the situation. Mr. Isaac is a jeweller by trade, and has resided in Leeds for a period of thirty-six years. In his business capacity he has been the medium of conveying bribes in the shape of presents to foremen. Latterly, he said, payments in cash have been substituted for presents of jewellery. Mr. Isaac spoke strongly of the injustice and injury caused by the fact that middlemen, having no knowledge whatever of the trade, were able, by means of bribery, to obtain orders, while practical tailors, who were not rich enough to bribe, were unable to get work. Many witnesses, and especially the last two mentioned, were of opinion that bribery is the root of the evil at Leeds, and that if it could be abolished sweating would practically disappear. Be that as it may, we entirely agree that the heads of firms would do well to look into this matter thoroughly for themselves, instead of entrusting everything to their foremen. We cannot doubt that great wrong is done to the working people by the corrupt influences which are exercised at their expense. Some complaints were brought before us with regard to the municipal contracts for police clothing. It appears that they were sent to London, and carried out at 30 per cent. less than the average prices. They were taken by a middleman and sub-let.

R. Burnett, 3C418.

The Bradford Woolcombers

EIGHT DOCUMENTS

I

Meeting of the Bradford Chamber of Commerce

ON December 30th, a meeting of the Council of the Bradford Chamber of Commerce was held, at which the following members were present:—Messrs. T. Arthur Duncan (president), G. Hoffmann (vice-president), the Mayor (Mr. T. Speight), G. S. Beaumont, Amos Crabtree, V. Edelstein, J. Ephraimson, J. Goodwin, W. B. Gordon, D. G. Law, Henry Muff, Arthur Priestman, H. D. Sichel, F. F. Steinthal, H. Sutcliffe, W. A. Whitehead, Alderman F. W. Jowett, David Wade, and F. Hooper (secretary).

After some preliminary business,

Mr. ARTHUR PRIESTMAN, in the absence of Mr. Smith Feather, opened a discussion on the recent sensational article in *Pearson's Magazine* on the conditions under which woolcombers work in Bradford. He said that the article in question had been widely read, and would seriously damage the reputation of Bradford as a commercial centre, so that it was the duty of the Chamber to take some cognisance of the statements there made. In the article there were six distinct charges. Firstly, the writer stated that the men who worked in combing-sheds on the night turn were so much reduced in physique that they weighed from two to three stone less than the average man. He also said that the wages earned were from 18s. to 20s. weekly, but as the men were idle for twenty-five weeks in the year, their average earnings were only 9s. to 10s. a week. Out of that a man had to support himself, his wife, and his children. As if that did not sound the depths of the woes of the operatives, the writer of the article referred to a new employer, who was only paying his men 15s. a week, which meant that a man's average earnings would be about 7s. 6d. a week. The article also contained a statement with reference to foul, poisonous yellow dust in combing-sheds, and spoke of it as if it were common throughout the trade. Probably the writer was referring to Persian wool or something of that kind. The heat in combing-sheds was said to be approximate to that in tropical regions, and the workers had to work without garments, thus giving rise to the picture which had, perhaps, attracted more attention than anything else in the article. The last charge was that when wool was being scoured the stench was so bad as to be " fit to knock you down." Those six charges were very grave ones upon the woolcombing industry of Bradford. It was quite possible for any one to attack any industry, however well organized and flourishing it might be. The Chamber, he suggested, ought to find out whether the charges in the article were true or false. If the statements were ignored, and treated with contempt, outsiders would think that they were correct, or that the woolcombers of Bradford were too indifferent to take any notice of them. If the charges were true, the Christmas festivities of the people of Bradford ought rather to have been days of mourning. He moved that a committee of three members of the Chamber be appointed to co-operate with three members of the Bradford Trades and Labour Council in investigating the accuracy of the statements, and to report to the Council at an early date. If the Council undertook the task alone, the report would be looked upon as merely a sectional one.

The MAYOR, in seconding the motion, said that even the extracts in the newspapers had convinced him that the statements in the article were a tissue of falsehoods from the beginning to the end. He had spoken to Mr. Shaftoe, whose name was connected with the article, and that gentleman had replied that the question of wages ought to be investigated. The question, however, was not one of wages, but of decency; and if the writer of the article had only mentioned his (the Mayor's) name, or that of some other woolcomber in whose establishment the atrocities were said to take place, the matter could have been taken up in proper form. In the article it was stated that the hours worked per week were from sixty-one to sixty-four. They all knew that they were only from fifty-four to fifty-six. He (the writer) also spoke of "bent old grandams of seventy" at the combing machines. He (the Mayor) questioned whether there was a woman to-day at a combing machine

APPENDIX 307

who was over sixty years of age. Then we were told that the heat in the combing-sheds was of a tropical character. He could only say that the writer of the article must have been in some very curious places. There were some establishments in congested districts where it was difficult to secure the admission of the proper amount of fresh air, and where there was not so much space as there ought to be. But he knew that some of the woolcombers who were thus circumstanced were leaving for more commodious and more healthy premises. The factory inspector testified that the progress in the woolcombing trade during the last ten years, in the direction of providing artificial ventilation, etc., was greater than he had thought to be possible. The inspector visited woolcombing establishments at all hours of the day and night, and he gave no warning of when he was coming. The whole article was a libel on the woolcombing trade of Bradford, and he (the Mayor) would be prepared to join in any steps which might be taken to give the lie to the false statements.[1]

Mr. WHITEHEAD thought that the matter was scarcely one for the Chamber of Commerce, because it was not their business to inquire into the truth of any sensational articles which might be written. A special commissioner, sent down by *The Textile Mercury*, had refuted the statements pretty thoroughly, and if the Press would give the same prominence to that refutation that they had done to the original allegations, no

---

[1] The Mayor has since retracted almost the whole of these remarks. Even the employers saw the futility of such a defence.

further denials would be necessary. Nine-tenths of the combing trade, at any rate, was conducted in a good and regular fashion. The buildings were lofty and of modern construction, and were under proper sanitary regulations. Moreover, it was untrue to say that the work was of an exceptionally laborious character. It required attention, but did not necessitate superhuman efforts, such as the writer of the article referred to. It was untrue to say that the atmosphere in a combing-shed was foul, and although it was necessarily hot, ample ventilation was provided in all modern sheds. Then, again, in many mills fans were placed over the washing bowls, to take away the hot air and the steam. Any one outside might think that the foul air expelled by the fans represented the atmosphere in which the men were working, when, as a matter of fact, the steam and foul air were sucked out of the building before they could diffuse about the room. The writer of the article referred in pitying tones to the physique of the workers, and called them "living skeletons" and "poor emaciated beings." Combing was an unskilled employment, and a certain proportion of elderly and almost infirm men were engaged in it. Perhaps they had been unfortunate in youth, and had not learned a trade, or they were not physically strong enough for heavier work. Those drifted into combing—some of them being old and broken down—because the work was comparatively light. He admitted that there was a proportion of broken-down men in combing-sheds whose physique was poor. But 90 per cent. of the men employed on the night turns were able-bodied men, who would bear comparison with those employed in cotton mills or any other textile industry. As to the women workers, the statements with reference to them were not correct, and many of the women were very much annoyed at the sketch which was published with the article. He (Mr. Whitehead) had never heard of anything of the sort in the trade before, and it was certainly not done at any of the large establishments. After the statements had been denied it would, he thought, be best to let the matter drop.

Alderman F. W. JOWETT said that he would not discuss the accuracy of the statements made in the article, although he had always regarded woolcombers on the night shifts with very great sympathy, and as much under the average in stamina. He had always thought that they had a great deal of reason to complain of the condition under which they worked. It would, he thought, be best for the Council to decide whether or not they would investigate the charges in the way proposed in the motion, and not to criticise the statements first. Mr. Jowett added that the article in *The Textile Mercury*, which spoke of wages being from 19s. to 30s. a week, was not much of a refutation of charges of so detailed a character.

Mr. CRABTREE thought that the matter was one for the combers who felt aggrieved to take up. When he first read the article, it seemed to be a gross exaggeration from beginning to end, and many of the statements were quite false.

The MAYOR said that, with Mr. Arthur Priestman's consent, he would withdraw from seconding the motion. He had only seconded it because he thought it was a unanimous expression of opinion on the part of the Council. He agreed that the matter was one for the woolcombers themselves to take up. If a letter were written from the Council to the Woolcombers' Association, calling their attention to the article, he, as President of that Association, would convene a meeting to deal with the matter. Some members of the Bradford Trades Council might be asked to meet the members of the Woolcombers' Association to discuss the subject.

Mr. PRIESTMAN assented to the Mayor's withdrawal, and the motion was seconded by Alderman F. W. Jowett.

Mr. W. H. MITCHELL suggested that any false impressions would be removed much more easily by an inquiry by the Chamber of Commerce than by woolcombers, who were directly interested in the matter.

Mr. SUTCLIFFE said that the remarks made at that Council meeting would show that the Chamber of Commerce denied the accuracy of the statements in the article. He thought that the woolcombers themselves ought to take any further steps which were deemed advisable.

Mr. EDELSTEIN thought that an independent inquiry would have the most effect.

Mr. HOFFMANN said that of the six charges in the article only one had reference to wages. Either the factory inspector or the medical officer of health, each of whom was independent alike of employers and employed, could say whether the other five charges were true or not. He thought if formal questions were submitted to those two gentlemen, and duly published in the newspapers, no further steps were necessary. He believed that the replies would be an absolute refutation of the six lies in the article.

The PRESIDENT agreed that the matter was rather one for woolcombers than for the Chamber as a whole. If the Woolcombers' Association would inquire into the matter, and would associate with them in the inquiry members of the Trades Council and the factory inspector and medical officer, the Council might safely let the matter drop.

The MAYOR moved that a letter be sent from the Council to the Woolcombers' Association asking them to deal with the matter. He would suggest to the Association that members of the Trades Council, the medical officer of health, and the factory inspector should be included in the inquiry.

Alderman JOWETT thought the woolcombers were not in the best position to make the inquiry.

Mr. CRABTREE seconded the Mayor's amendment, which was carried by 12 votes to 4, the minority consisting of Mr. Muff, Mr. Mitchell, Mr. Arthur Priestman, and Alderman Jowett.

The Council then separated.

II

Meeting of the Trades and Labour Council

LAST Tuesday night a meeting of the Bradford and District Trades and Labour Council was held in the Engineers' Rooms, Sackville Street, Bradford, Mr. RALPH HARVEY presiding over a large attendance of delegates.

The correspondence included a letter from the Town Clerk of Bradford (Mr. G. McGuire), stating that a meeting would be held in the Mayor's Parlour on Thursday afternoon next, to inquire into the truth of the allegations contained in a recent article in *Pearson's Magazine*, as to the conditions of employment in woolcombing establishments. The letter further stated that the medical officer of health (Dr. Evans) and the factory inspector had been asked to be present at the meeting, and asked if a member of the Trades Council would also attend in order to give a representative statement as to the workers' views on the statements contained in the article.

Mr. S. SHAFTOE (secretary of the Machine Woolcombers' Union) said that some of the statements contained in the article in question had been obtained from him, and were correct, but others, derived from outside sources, were exaggerated.[1] The Mayor of Bradford, however, had described the article as a tissue of falsehoods, and had said, for example, that woolcombers only worked from fifty-four to fifty-six hours per

---

[1] In a letter to the publisher of this book, dated Feb. 12, 1897, Mr. Shaftoe acknowledges the substantial accuracy of my account, whilst objecting to the illustration representing a half-nude woman which accompanied the article—an illustration with which I had nothing to do. "Mr. Sherard's article in the Christmas Number of *Pearson's Magazine* . . . gives all the information that can possibly be given in reference to the wages and other conditions of labour in the Industry of Machine Woolcombing."

week, instead of from sixty to sixty-four as the writer had stated. It is true that, in consequence of the Factory Acts, the hours of the operatives employed in woolcombing establishments during the day did not exceed fifty-six and a half weekly, but men employed on the night shifts had at times to work from sixty to sixty-three hours in one week. *The Textile Mercury* had published an article combating the statements made in the magazine, and had asked him (Mr. Shaftoe) to grant an interview to their representative. The publication of the first article, however, had resulted in his receiving so much correspondence and humbug that he had declined (laughter). In *The Textile Mercury*. however—a paper owned by employers—the wages of woolcombers were stated to vary from 19s. to 32s. weekly, instead of from 17s. to 23s. Could any one show him a woolcomber who exceeded 26s. a week? (A voice: "They have included the overlookers.") The commission woolcombers in Bradford found fault with Mr. Sherard for his exaggerated statements in the magazine, but not with *The Textile Mercury* for making such audacious allegations as to the wages which were paid. Any inquiry which was undertaken ought to be a fair and full one, and should not be carried out in a half-hearted fashion. If any factory inspector was to meet the masters he hoped that it would be Mr. Beaumont, of whose veracity he had no doubt, and who was conversant with the facts, instead of a gentleman newly appointed to the post. The Mayor had said that they wanted an inquiry, not into the question of wages, but of decency.

He (Mr. Shaftoe) still maintained, as he had always done, that low wages were demoralising, and that where low wages were paid decency could not be expected (hear, hear). The Woolcombers' Union were holding a special meeting to consider the article before long, and after that gathering they would be in a position to elect two operatives, who could go before the masters and say which statements were true and which were incorrect. He suggested that a proper way to hold an inquiry into the matter would be for it to be undertaken by a committee of twelve members, consisting of three delegates from each of four bodies—the Trades Council, the Woolcombers' Union, the Chamber of Commerce, and the Master Woolcombers' Association, with the factory inspector (Mr. Beaumont) and the medical officer of health (Dr. Evans). The workpeople admitted that some of the statements which the article contained were overdrawn, but they were prepared to point out which were the incorrect statements. not to have the article repudiated altogether. He moved—

That the Secretary of the Council (Alderman F. W. Jowett) write to the Mayor of Bradford, informing him that the Council are willing to join in an independent inquiry into the statements contained in the article referred to, and suggesting that the committee should be constituted as follows:—Three members of the Trades Council, three operatives from the Woolcombers' Union, three members of the Chamber of Commerce, and three members of the Master Woolcombers' Association, with the

APPENDIX 315

medical officer of health (Dr. Evans) and the factory inspector (Mr. Beaumont).

Mr. PAUL BLAND, in seconding the motion, said that his experience had led him to believe that many of the statements in the article were quite true.

Mr. W. H. DREW suggested that, if the master woolcombers would not undertake an inquiry on the lines suggested by Mr. Shaftoe, the Council ought to investigate the matter themselves. Their findings would only be *ex parte* in the same sense as the decisions of the Woolcombers' Association inquiry would be.

Mr. SHAFTOE said that if the employers let the matter drop he would not object to doing the same. He, however, accepted Mr. Drew's suggestion as a rider to his motion.

The resolution, with the rider suggested by Mr. Drew, was adopted unanimously. It was understood that the motion implied a refusal of the invitation contained in the Town Clerk's letter.

III

Extract from Annual Report of the Bradford Chamber of Commerce

IN an article which appeared in one of the monthly magazines, certain disparaging statements were made concerning the Bradford Woolcombing Industry, and the article formed the subject of a discussion at a Council meeting held on the 30th December last. Several members of the Council disputed the accuracy of the statements in question, and on the suggestion of the Mayor (Mr. Thomas Speight), the Council recommended the Woolcombers' Association to investigate the matter. The following letter from the Mayor has since been received :—

MAYOR'S PARLOUR, TOWN HALL,
BRADFORD,

DEAR SIR,—   *7th January,* 1897.

In accordance with the recommendation conveyed to me in your letter of the 31st ultimo, I invited members of the Woolcombers' Association, the Factory Inspector, the Medical Officer of Health, and representatives of the Trades and Labour Council, to attend a conference in my rooms this afternoon to consider the question of making a statement on behalf of the trade in reply to the article on Woolcombing, which appeared in the December number of *Pearson's Magazine.*

I regret to state that the Factory Inspector and the Trades and Labour Council declined to take part in the conference.

Dr. Evans, the Medical Officer of Health for the Borough of Bradford, was present, and stated that in reference to the sanitation of the woolcombing establishments the Factory Acts are in full operation, and that these establishments bear favourable comparison with other factories and workshops in the Borough.

I have to inform you that the following resolution was unanimously agreed to by the meeting :

" That a reply be sent to the Chamber of Commerce stating that the magazine article to which they refer is so misleading and contains so many misrepresentations of facts that we do not consider it worthy of further notice."   I am, Dear Sir,

Yours faithfully,
THOS. SPEIGHT, *Mayor.*

FREDK. HOOPER, Esq.,
Secretary, Chamber of Commerce, Exchange, Bradford.

APPENDIX

IV

Letter from a Member of the Bradford Chamber of Commerce [1]

ROOKWOOD, BRADFORD,
YORKS,
January 29*th*, 1897.

SIR,—
In reply to your letter (without date) from St. Ives', I beg to state that the paragraph in the *Bradford Observer* of December 31st is not an accurate report of the remarks that fell from my lips during the discussion in question.

It can be clearly seen from the context even of this report that I was in favour of getting an investigation of the matter by the most impartial authorities; and I personally, not being interested in woolcombing, gave no opinion on the merits of the question.

You may be sure that I, as Chairman of the Board of Conciliation, should not be likely to use any offensive expressions with reference to any question between Capital and Labour.

If you are not satisfied with the above explanation, you may of course take such proceedings as you may think fit to do.

Yours sincerely,
G. HOFFMANN.

ROBERT H SHERARD, Esq.,
4, Bellair Terrace,
St. Ives.

---

[1] This letter was written in answer to a letter which I wrote to Colonel Hoffmann, who had spoken of the "six lies" in my article. I selected him at hazard, to test how far the members of the Bradford Chamber of Commerce were prepared to stand by their statements.

V

A Conference of the Masters

"An important conference of Bradford woolcombers was held this afternoon in the Mayor's Parlour at the Town Hall relative to the charges contained in the article in a London magazine on 'The White Slaves of England.' The Mayor (Mr. T. Speight), as President of the Woolcombers' Association, occupied the chair. The meeting was a thoroughly representative one, about fourteen combers being present, including Mr. T. Shaw and Mr. J. Hill. Others present also were Mr. Ald. W. Willis Wood, Mr. McGuire (Town Clerk), and Dr. Evans (Medical Officer of Health). No representative of the Bradford Trades and Labour Council put in an appearance. The meeting was private, but we are in a position to state that it was decided to draw up a letter to the Chamber of Commerce in reply to the suggestion that the conference should be held. We understand also that the suggestion of the Trades and Labour Council that the Committee should be constituted of three members each of that Council, of the Chamber of Commerce, of the Woolcombers' Association, and three representatives from the Woolcombers' Union, was considered at some length, but was not entertained."—*Bradford Telegraph*, Jan. 7th.

VI

The Decision arrived at

"The Bradford Master Woolcombers' Association has decided to take no further action for the refutation of the article in *Pearson's Magazine*, and it is understood that the matter will now drop as far as all parties are concerned."—*Bradford Telegraph*, Jan. 14th.

APPENDIX 319

VII

A Meeting of the Operatives

"A meeting of the Bradford and District Machine Woolcombers' (Operatives) Association was held on Saturday, for the purpose of discussing the article which appeared recently in a monthly magazine on the conditions of woolcombing in Bradford. The meeting lasted about two hours, the statements in the article being taken up and considered *seriatim*. The effect of the discussion was, it is reported, to show the opinion of the meeting that, apart from the illustration of a woman at work in a half-naked condition, which was repudiated, the article was substantially true. A resolution was adopted to this effect, and Mr. S. Shaftoe, the Secretary of the Association, was instructed to report the conclusions at which the Association had arrived to the Council of the Chamber of Commerce. It was also resolved to lay the matter before the Bradford and District Trades and Labour Council, with a view to placing before them materials for forming a judgment on the matter. To this end, five persons (three male and two female) were appointed to give evidence before the Council, on which the Association has a permanent representation of four delegates."—*Bradford Telegraph*, Jan. 18th.

VIII

The Question once more before the Bradford Chamber of Commerce

"An ordinary Council meeting of this Chamber was held at the Exchange this morning, Mr. T. A. Duncan, the retiring president, presiding *pro tem*. Others present were Messrs. G. Hoffmann, G. S. Beaumont, Amos Crabtree, Victor Edelstein, Julius Ephraimson, Smith Feather, Herbert A. Foster, B. Cohen, J. A.

Godwin, William B. Gordon, J. C. Horsfall, Albert H. Illingworth, W. H. Mitchell, Arthur Priestman, H. D. Sichel, F. F. Steinthal, Henry Sutcliffe, W. A. Whitehead, David Wade, F. Illingworth, William Watson, and F. Hooper (Secretary).

"After other business, the following was dealt with :

"The Machine Woolcombers' Association wrote in reference to the recent magazine article on the ' White Slaves' question that, in the opinion of the Association, the statements made in the article were substantially true.

"Mr. Smith Feather moved that the letter be laid under the table. (Laughter.)

"It was eventually agreed to allow the letter to lie on the table."—*Bradford Telegraph*, Jan. 27th.

Is any comment needed on the above? Do not the eight documents tell their story very plainly? The Mayor of Bradford (a woolcomber himself), the Bradford Chamber of Commerce, the Bradford Master Woolcombers' Association, blusteringly clamour for an inquiry. After one or two secret conferences they agree to let the matter drop, although in the meanwhile the Operatives' Association has also held an inquiry, and confirms the accuracy of my statements. The insolent and contemptible treatment awarded to the letter from the Operatives' Association by the Bradford Chamber of Commerce is reported above. The Mayor at the first meeting regretted that the case could not be brought into court. I immediately afforded the Master Woolcombers an opportunity of defending themselves before a jury by asking one of the members of the Chamber of Commerce, who had described me as a liar, for the name of a solicitor who would accept service on his behalf in an action for slander. He replied by saying that he had been inaccurately reported. I confidently leave the public to judge between me and the Bradford Master Woolcombers.

I must add that the *Bradford Telegraph*, from which the above extracts are taken, is an anti-Unionist paper, which has attacked me persistently during the whole controversy.

"The Textile Mercury" and The Woolcombers

THE article in *The Textile Mercury*, to which reference was made at the meetings both of the Bradford Chamber of Commerce and of the Trades Council, appeared in the issue of that journal for December 26th of last year, under the heading—

"THE WHITE SLAVES OF ENGLAND
MORE LIBELS REFUTED"

and was written by the same person who "followed closely on the heels" of Mr. Robert Machray in Leeds when that gentleman was collecting optimistic data for his article on the "Gates and Pillars of the Empire." In this instance he appears to have been more successful as a tracker, and amongst other information discovered the hotel at which I stayed whilst in Bradford, and the striking fact that on one occasion I offered a pint of beer and a piece of bread and cheese to a poor old woolcomber who had called on me there by appointment. I am, unfortunately, unable to quote the whole article *in extenso*. It is very long, and it contains passages concerning myself, with which I propose to deal otherwise than by quotation. I will essay, however, to give the gist of this refutation.

Before doing so, it will be edifying to the reader to take cognizance of an editorial note in the same issue. The editor writes:—

" We invite the attention of our readers to our leading article this week. Perhaps some of them may have read a series of papers appearing in *Pearson's Magazine* under the title of ' The White Slaves of England.' *The statements in the last one are so extraordinary that they at once roused in our mind a strong suspicion that they could not be true.* To set the matter at rest, we despatched a gentleman of *The Textile Mercury* editorial staff to follow, as far as could be discovered, ' Pearson's ' contributor over the same ground. This he did, and the story is told in the article referred to."

I have italicized the passage to which I wish to draw attention. Here we have the editor of a paper enjoying the "largest textile circulation," who confesses his ignorance of the conditions of labour in the principal textile industry in England. He has suspicions that my statements were not true, and despatches a gentleman of the editorial staff to investigate the matter, a Stanley to that dark and remote region of which the name is Bradford, to inquire into the habits and methods of living of a little known race called Woolcombers.

The one fact above all others which I endeavoured to prove out of the mouths of the workers themselves was that the Bradford woolcombers are shamefully underpaid. This is the head and front of their grievance, for from this all their trouble proceeds. As Mr. Shaftoe remarked : " Low wages are demoralizing." The payment per hour is for women 2½d., and for men 3¾d.

The commissioner of *The Textile Mercury* deals at length with the question of wages. His statements have been described as "audacious allegations" by the Bradford Labour Associations. I will not so characterize them. I will simply quote his words, and having commented upon them, leave the reader to judge for himself. I italicize passages to which I wish to call particular attention.

" The labour employed in woolcombing is, as Mr. Sherard says, of the unskilled order, and for work of that class the wages paid are very fair. There is very little physical exertion required, as is proved by the fact that the work, which during the night-time is carried on by men earning 18s. or 20s. a week, is easily performed during the day by women and girls at 12s. to 13s. a week. *Factory Act regulations alone preventing the whole of the operations from being carried out by female labour.* In the combe-rooms at Bradford the girls employed in gilling earn 12s. to 12s. 6d. a week, and some get 13s. Men are employed in the card-room, where the earnings range from 19s. to 30s., the latter being paid to hands in responsible positions. The heads of two large establishments on whom I called for information allowed me to make extracts freely from their wage-books, and one firm, employing about 1,400 hands, has, I find, a number of men in the card-room getting from 24s. to 26s. a week, the others earning from 19s. to 24s., and boys 12s. These are the standard wages. Many men, however, do not earn these amounts, simply because they refuse to work a full week. The night-foreman at one large establishment informs me that during busy times some of the hands will say, 'Oh! be ——d to this. I'm gooin t' have a day off.' I have no desire, however, to cast a reflection upon the operative woolcombers as a body. They include a large number of steady, sober and thrifty men, some of whom own the houses they live in. Mr. Sherard has not sought for his facts among workers of this stamp, but appears to have interrogated the 'submerged tenth' of the trade. One of his witnesses, whom I will not particularise, went to the works recently in a very drunken condition, and for fear of his injuring himself was allowed to sleep off the effects of his too copious potations. Mr. Sherard makes a good deal of his evidence, which under the circumstances can scarcely be regarded as of value. *Many of the night-men, with whom the article in 'Pearson's' chiefly deals, belong to that improvident class whose members would be poor no matter how large their earnings.* Until recently they were in the habit of demanding their wages at one establishment when only one or two nights' pay were due, in order to indulge in a drinking bout, and employers who refused to pay before the end of the week have been threatened with violence at the hands of these gentry. In one of the factories visited in preparing the material for this article, the standard wages for night work are 21s. 6d. Turning over the wage-book at random, *I picked out a man whose earnings for March were 17s. 2d., 12s. 10d., 8s. 7d., 12s. 2d., and 17s. 10d.*, during five successive weeks. As work was plentiful during the whole of this period, and other men had good wages throughout, the poor weeks in the foregoing list *would be due to illness or some other cause.* In April and succeeding months the weekly earnings of the same man were as follows:—21s. 6d., 21s. 6d., 17s. 2d., 17s. 2d., 17s. 2d., 8s. 7d., 21s. 6d., an average for the seven weeks of 17s. 9d. Then in June comes a run of five weeks at 21s. 6d., followed in September and October by seven weeks in which the earnings were never below that amount. A glance at other names showed that a large number of men were earning over 21s. during the period mentioned. An old man who simply shakes the wool as it comes from the wash bowl gets 17s. 6d. a week for his services: and in another part of the works I saw girls standing with folded arms watching the re-combing of dyed wool at 11s. 6d. to 12s. a week, their services being only required when ends break, which is not often."

So, but for the Factory Act, the Bradford employers would put women on the night-shifts, and work them from 5.30 p.m. to 6 a.m. for five days in the week for 12s. to 13s.

As to the story about the man who went to work drunk—I presume it is poor old Berry who is referred to—it has been denied in another journal, and even were it true, it reflects discredit on the foreman rather than on the man.

But what I like best of all in the above is the

APPENDIX 327

quotation from the wage-book. In March this man earned an average of 13s. 8d. a week. It is obvious that he did all the work that was found for him to do. If he had been ill during the "poor weeks," he could not have earned 12s. 10d. in one week, or 8s. 7d. in another. No sick man can work 26 hours in one week or 36 hours in the next. In April and May he earned £6 4s. 7d. April and May consist of 61 days, or 9 woolcomber's weeks. Sixty-one days divided by seven gives eight weeks and five-sevenths. The five-sevenths (or five days) represent a woolcomber's week. So dividing the £6 4s. 7d. by nine, we find that his average weekly earnings were 13s. 10d. In June he earned 21s. 6d. a week. In July and August he earned nothing. He was probably at the seaside, or on the moors. In September and October he earned £7 10s. 6d. Dividing this again by nine, we get an average of 16s. 6d. a week.

Totalling up his earnings as follows:—

	£	s.	d.
In March	3	8	7
In April and May	6	4	7
In June	5	7	6
In July and August	0	0	0
In September and October	7	10	6
Summa Summarum	£22	11	2

In these eight months there are thirty-five weeks, so that his average income per week during that period was 11s. 9d.—eleven shillings and ninepence. Ah, but he was not working all the time. No, he was not. He was larking during the slack weeks, with his hands in his pockets and his back to the wall, and. God help him, his waist-strap tightly drawn. He was a man anxious to work, zealous at work—the figures show that—and all his zeal and industry could bring him was an income of eleven shillings and ninepence a week. As work is irregular and intermittent in the combing sheds, and as the combers must dance attendance on their employers, work or no work, under penalty of being discarded—retainers without retaining fees—so that they are unable to seek temporary employment elsewhere, the wages should be such that, taking the whole year, the combers should have a sufficient weekly income. As it is, in Bradford, as Mr. Shaftoe has stated, the average weekly income of a woolcomber does not exceed 14s. I persist in describing this as sweating.

The "refutation" continues with an account of my interview with Mr. Shaftoe, who declined to receive *The Textile Mercury's* commissioner. Since my article has appeared, Mr. Shaftoe has been assailed on all sides, and in self-protection has made it public that he is responsible only for such information as he gave me officially, in the Woolcombers' club-room. That is so, nor have I ever attributed anything else to him. The commissioner writes:—

"Even the secretary of the Woolcombers' Association, Mr. Sam Shaftoe, J.P., to whom Mr. Sherard appealed for information, feels impelled to repudiate his connection with the matter."

And lower down, as illustrating Mr. Shaftoe's repudiation :—

APPENDIX

"The history of Mr. Sherard's 'investigation' as given by Mr. Shaftoe is interesting. In the early part of this year he made his appearance at the house of the latter, and introduced himself as a correspondent on behalf of *Pearson's Monthly Magazine*, commissioned by the proprietors of that magazine to visit several towns with a view of making inquiry as to wages paid and other conditions of labour in special industries. He stated that he had been specially recommended to see Mr. Shaftoe in reference to the wages paid, the hours of labour, and other conditions under which the operatives in the woolcombing business had to work. Having been interviewed scores of times during his lifetime on questions of this kind, Mr. Shaftoe naturally complied with his request, and took him down to the club-room, and took out the schedule of wages paid by several important firms of the town, saying, 'You will see for yourself from these schedules, and also the evidence given by the operatives themselves before the Labour Commission, the rate of wages paid and hours worked, and all other conditions of labour in this special industry.' Mr. Shaftoe is not himself a woolcomber, being engaged in the skip trade; but he sides with Mr. Sherard in many of his assertions. He told him, for instance, that he considered people employed in woolcombing the worst paid for their labour of any class of operatives under the sun, and taking their wages and all other conditions under which they had to work into consideration, he looked upon them as the white slaves of the textile industry of either Yorkshire or Lancashire, and that he still maintains. Mr.

Sherard then asked Mr. Shaftoe if he could get him through any of the woolcombing premises at midnight, to see the internal condition of the combing-shed for himself. His reply was that he did not feel disposed to have anything to do with that business, upon which the 'White Slave' imaginator said that he would see to it himself and take illustrations to supplement his article."

The "White Slave imaginator" (whatever that may be) most certainly never said that he would take illustrations to supplement his article. I had as little to do with that part of the work as with the printing of the magazine.

The rest of the articles is made up of various statements, the value of which as refutations may be judged by the following :—

"He speaks of the yellow dust and the stench in the woolcombing establishments. I have been through several, and failed to notice anything of the kind. As a matter of fact woolcombing is an exceptionally light and healthy occupation, and compared, for instance, with the life of seamen in the merchant service who have to brave the fury of the gales round Cape Horn, at £3 a month, the Bradford woolcombers are well off."

"A child could do the work equally well" (*i.e.* a child could work ten hours a day).

And so on, and so on.

My article appeared on December 1st. The above "refutation" appeared on December 26th. Nothing had been said in the Bradford papers in

APPENDIX

the meanwhile. Indeed, the editor of *The Textile Mercury* comments upon this significant fact in the following terms :—

"The article by our Special Commissioner, which appeared in these columns last week, has received widespread attention in Bradford, the daily papers of the worsted district making lengthy quotations from *The Textile Mercury*. To the individual of average intelligence it will seem a very strange thing indeed that the task undertaken voluntarily by the management of this journal was not discharged by some of the Yorkshire newspapers immediately after the publication of the glaring inaccuracies which have been the subject of so much comment of late. Even now the admissions made by *The Bradford Observer* are of such a character that one is forced to the conclusion that they are made unwillingly."

The Bradford Woolcombers and their Wages

I AM indebted to the Special Commissioner of *The Yorkshire Factory Times*, which has throughout shown itself in sympathy with the unfortunate workers in the "devil's hoils" (as the combers call the combing-sheds) for the following amplifications of my statements about the wages paid to these workers. I beg my readers to compare them with the quotations of *The Textile Mercury*.

From the issue of *The Factory Times* of Jan. 8th, 1897, I quote the subjoined table of wages, "which," so runs the writer's introduction, "Mr. Shaftoe assures your Commissioner is by no means an average one, but that obtaining in one of the best paid firms of the town.

Table of Wages.

Washhouse (men only) during the night :— £ s. d.
Bowl minders, 3 bowls 1 2 0
„ „ feeders 0 18 0
During the day :—
Bowl minders, 3 bowls 1 0 0
„ „ feeders 0 14 0

Strippers and grinders (men, each of whom has to attend 12 cards and 2 grinders), jobbers :—Men, night, £1 2s. for 11 Botany cards or 6 English ; day turn, £1 for the same quantity of machinery.

Card feeders, by hopper and hand (men), 18s. for 6 cards at night ; (women), 12s. for 6 cards at day.

APPENDIX

Back-end minders by balling head or coiler cans:—
Men, at night, 19s. for 6 English cards, and 18s. for 11 Botany; women, day, 12s. for 6 English cards, and 12s. for 11 Botany.

Burr takers-out (men), 18s. for 11 cards at night, and 14s. for 11 cards at day.

Shoddy willeyers (men), 18s. day.

Wool runners (men), £1 for 11 cards at night; 18s. for 11 cards at day.

Backwash minders, and number of backwashers each person has to attend to:—Men, £1 for 1 backward and strong box (night); 12s. for ditto (day).

	£	s.	d.
Finishing box minders, men, night,			
English (4 boxes)	0	19	0
Medium (2 boxes)	0	18	0
Women, day, English (4 boxes)	0	12	0
,, ,, Medium (2 boxes)	0	12	0
Comb Minders, men, night, English (for 2 combs)	1	3	0
Medium	1	2	0
Botany	1	0	0
Women, day, English (for 2 combs)	0	14	0
,, ,, Medium	0	12	6
,, ,, Botany	0	12	6
Strong Gill box minders, men, night,			
Botany (for 2 boxes)	0	18	0
Medium	0	18	0
English (for 4 boxes)	0	19	0
Women, day, English	0	12	0
,, ,, Botany	0	12	0
Making-up Box minders, men, night	0	18	0
,, ,, ,, women, day	0	12	0
Men Jobbers, night, English	1	6	0
,, ,, ,, Botany	1	4	0
,, ,, day, English	1	0	0
,, ,, ,, Botany	1	0	0
One man taking noils and cans out of 4 combs	1	0	0

The writer points out that "the figures refer to wages earned when the worker has put in a full week's work—that is 56½ hours on the day turn, and 63¾ hours on the night turn," and concludes :—

"When the writers who put pen to paper can go over these facts, which conclusively prove that the industry is not one of easy work, that it is underpaid, that not only does the heat compel men and women to divest themselves of as much of their clothing as decency permits, that those engaged in the trade on the night turn work 12¼ hours, many of them with no cessation for meals; then and then only will the time come for such writers as Mr. Sherard to cease denouncing the horrid conditions under which the bulk of the wealth of Bradford's princes has been made."

On Saturday, January 16th, 1897, a meeting of woolcombers was held at the clubroom, which I have described. The Special Commissioner of *The Factory Times* was present, and gives in the issue of that paper of January 22nd a long and most interesting account of the way in which the operatives discussed my article and the "refutation" in *The Textile Mercury*. I have only room for the statements made by the workpeople themselves, when asked by the Chairman for their wages' averages.

"It was not to be expected that your woolcomber, 'incapable and lacking intellectuality,' as his employer asserts, was prepared for this. Fortunately one man, wise in his generation, had a black and white statement, and capable heads figured up his totals. What would you, my masters? He was a wealthy man. For seventy-one weeks his average earnings were 9s. 10d.

APPENDIX

"Another had a firm conviction that 10s. per week was as much as he had earned. A third went a little higher; he had earned 12s. Another said his wage occasionally ran up to 14s., but from that, as a set-off, there were the weeks when he had no wages; a full week for him was a memory of the past. A fourth was willing to risk ten thousand to one that at a much-belauded firm the whole of the men employed, excepting the jobber, had not averaged 10s. per week the whole of the past year. Finally (naming the firm) one fine, intelligent man held that the average had not reached 8s.; and so the tale went round."

In the issue of January 1st, the same writer had already published certain statements about the wages earned by the woolcombers.

From his article describing the manner in which the "refutation" in *The Textile Mercury* was received by the operatives, I clip the following paragraph:—

"The pity is that *The Textile Mercury* is not read by the woolcombers, or that this employers' journal did not pursue its investigations away from the surveillance of foremen and managers. 'Why was it not a part of the exposure to reveal what able-bodied men receive for working during the day, and so compare the labour price of men and women doing equally the same work?' asked one of the intelligent men I queried on this subject. Echo asks why. 'Dick Delaney's donkey would use his heels upon the man who told him that the average wage of the average woolcomber, even for the seven weeks quoted, was 17s. 9d.,' said a second. 'More like 7s. 9d., take the year round,' added a third; but all were agreed that, whilst it would be difficult to present figures for confirmation of their estimate, it was not too much to say that the average yearly earnings of the average woolcomber were not more than £26."

The White-Lead Workers

I SUBJOIN a few extracts from the Report to the Home Secretary from the Departmental Committee on the various Lead Industries. This Report [C. 7239] is published by Eyre & Spottiswoode, price 3d., from whom also the Minutes of Evidence, Appendices, and Index may be obtained, price, post-free. 4s. 1d.

The Committee was appointed April, 1893, and was composed of :—

James Henderson [1] (Chairman), Her Majesty's Superintending Inspector of Factories.

Thomas Oliver, M.D., F.R.C.P., Physician to the Infirmary, Newcastle-upon-Tyne.

Arthur Pillans Laurie, Fellow of King's College, Cambridge.

Edward Gould, Her Majesty's Superintending Inspector of Factories.

Henry James Cameron, Her Majesty's Inspector of Factories.

Harold John Tennant, Assistant Private Secretary to the Secretary of State and Secretary to the Committee.

The Committee visited 46 works, and examined 184 witnesses. It describes, in the first place,

[1] Mr. Henderson died on the 15th of July following, and Mr. E. Gould was elected Chairman in his place.

APPENDIX

the manufacture of white lead, by the old Dutch process, which gives the best commercial results.

As I have described this process in the chapter on the White Lead Workers, it is unnecessary to repeat it here. I wish, however, to quote paragraph *d* of this description, as confirming a statement of mine which has been contested.

(*d*) The filling is done through a rectangular opening in the middle of one of the sides of the stack, which is closed by boards as the stack gets filled. As the floors in the stack rise higher and higher, the tan, pots, wickets, and boards have to be carried up to greater and greater heights. This carrying is very generally done by women, who have to carry on their heads from 30 to 50 pounds of lead at a time up ladders 10 to 15 feet high. When the stack is full, ventilating shafts having been left at each corner of the stack, it is closed up and left to itself for periods of from 10 to 15 or more weeks. During this time the conversion of the blue lead into white lead (corrosion) takes place.

I refer the reader to the statement made to me by the poor old woman, by the side of whose death-bed I passed an hour in the Newcastle Workhouse.

The Committee proceeds to describe the

EFFECTS OF LEAD.

8 (*a*). It is known that if lead (in any form), even in what may be called infinitesimal quantities, gains entrance into the system for a lengthened period, by such channels as the stomach, by swallowing lead dust in the saliva, or through the medium of food or drink: by the respiratory organs, as by the inhalation of dust; or

through the skin, there is developed a series of symptoms, the most frequent of which is colic. Nearly all the individuals engaged in factories where lead or its compounds are manipulated look pale, and it is this bloodlessness, and the presence of a blue line along the margin of the gums, close to the teeth, that herald the other symptoms of *plumbism*.

(*b*) A form of paralysis known as wrist-drop, or lead palsy, occasionally affects the hands of the operatives. There is, in addition, a form of acute lead poisoning, most frequently met with in young girls from 18 to 24 years of age, which is suddenly developed, and is extremely fatal. In it the first complaint is headache, followed, sooner or later, by convulsions and unconsciousness. Death often terminates such a case within three days.[1] In some cases of recovery from convulsions total blindness remains.

9. There has been considerable doubt as to the channels by which the poison enters the system. The Committee have taken much evidence on this subject, and have arrived at the conclusion—(*a*) that carbonate of lead may be absorbed through the pores of the skin, and that the chance of this is much increased during perspiration and where there is any friction between the skin and the clothing; (*b*) that minute portions of lead are carried by the hands, under and round the nails, etc., on to the food, and so into the stomach; (*c*) but that the most usual manner is by the inhalation of the lead dust. Some of this becomes dissolved in the alkaline secretions of the mouth, and is swallowed with the saliva, thus finding its way to the stomach. Other particles of dust are carried to the lungs, where they are rendered soluble and absorbed by the blood.

Dealing with the Danger of Working, the Committee (par. 13)—"After duly considering

[1] *Cf.* case of Elizabeth Ryan, aged 19, amongst others of recent occurrence.

APPENDIX

all the evidence, have come to the conclusion that (*a*) women are more susceptible to lead-poisoning than men, and (*b*) young girls than full-grown women. On an analysis of the evidence of the doctors whom they have examined, it will be found that on question (*a*) this is the opinion of eight out of thirteen, and that only four dissent; while on (*b*) fourteen doctors agree, while three disagree."

Then follow a list of recommendations. I quote two of these:

18. Having regard to the fact that in all parts of a white lead factory where the old Dutch process is in use, there must be some lead-dust in suspension in the atmosphere, the Committee recommend that no girl under the age of 20 be employed in such a factory. In order that this recommendation may be the better executed, the Committee advise that every woman, before being passed by the doctor and taken on by the foreman, be compelled to produce a certificate either of birth or of baptism, so that her age may be accurately ascertained.

They recommend that the procuring of these certificates be facilitated in every way, and that the charge for them be made the same for women as it is at present for young persons under the age of 16 employed in factories or workshops, namely, sixpence.

19. The Committee further recommend that no woman be employed in the white-beds, the rollers, the washbecks, the stoves, or in packing dry white lead, and that these departments should consequently be worked in future only by adult males.

Having regard to the drastic nature of the proposed change, they would suggest that this provision should not come into force until 1st January, 1896.

The Committee hope that the efforts of some of the

manufacturers to devise mechanical means for stacking, stripping, drying and packing will be emulated by others, so that eventually an adequate and successful process may be in general use.

My visit to Newcastle took place in the spring of 1896. If these recommendations had been followed in the meanwhile, the lives of Elizabeth Ryan and her sisters in misfortune might have been saved.

The White-Lead Workers

AND

THE DEPARTMENTAL COMMITTEE'S REPORT

THE Minutes of Evidence taken before the Departmental Committee on the various Lead Industries, whose report has been referred to previously, are published in a Blue Book (dated 1894, price 3s. 7d.) which contains 445 pages. As it is impossible in a work of this description to quote at length the various questions and answers bearing on the points referred to in my article, I content myself with re-printing from the index to this Blue Book the summaries of the evidence given by each witness on the questions in which we are particularly interested. These summaries are very eloquent.

BLINDNESS.

Almost utter absence of blindness from lead noticeable of late, *Dr. Whammond*, 1352-4.

Had several cases, generally young women, four or five years ago, *ib.*, 1353-6.

Cases of blindness among lead workers are known, *Dr. Yoakley*, 1852-9.

Saw a girl blind through lead, 15 or 16 years ago; she had fits previously, *Dr. Hay*, 3168-72.

CHILDREN OF LEAD WORKERS.

Mary Roche had four children after going into a lead factory; one was stillborn, one subject to epileptic convulsions, and two died in convulsions shortly after birth, *Dr. Forbes*, 31–2.
Previously had two healthy children, *ib.*
Occasionally meets with a child suffering from convulsions, possibly due to mother having worked in a lead factory, *Dr. Baumgartner*, 954.
Had ten; health never suffered through working in lead, *Anderson*, 1043–5.
Had three children : two died in infancy, *Killoran*, 1083–7.
If a woman works in lead during pregnancy, child is, as a rule, weakly, *Dr. Whamond*, 1374–6.
Never had any children or miscarriages, *Fountain*, 1409–11.
Had two children; one died when six months old, *Scott*, 1455–9.
Had five children; first and last died in infancy, *Mills*, 1515–7.
Never had any children, *Mack*, 1546–7.
Had three; two died, but not through lead, *Knight*, 1585–96.
Had two; both are living, *Long*, 1615–6.
Working in lead affects the children, *Dr. Yoakley*, 1838.
They are puny, and generally die in convulsions, *ib.*, 1839–41.
Consequences disastrous where both father and mother are lead workers, *ib.*, 1844.
Lead is blamed for death of children in convulsions, *Dr. Newton*, 1962.
Had four; did not lose any, no miscarriages, *MacVey*, 2391–3.
Babies nursed by lead workers must suffer, *Dr. Scott*, 3078.

APPENDIX 343

Had four children; two died, but not of fits, *Young*, 3243-6.
Lost four children, all young; one died in convulsions, *Hultum*, 4003-7.
One born since entering lead works; is as healthy as anybody's, *ib.*, 4009-11.
Had one child: it died of convulsions, *Cox*, 4095-8.
Had four children: three died in infancy, one of convulsions, *Oliver*, 4132-40.
Was working at a laundry then, *ib.*, 4141-4.
Lost four, in infancy, since working in lead works, *Doyle*, 4324-32.
Lost three children out of four; they died of convulsions, or something on the brain, *Peterie*, 4406-13.
Had two; one died in convulsive fits, *Ford*, 4961-4.
Had two, both dead-born, *Walders*, 6212-4.
Had seven, lost two; one died at a month old of convulsions, *Norris*, 6245-8.
Had eight; two died, but not of convulsions, *Brown*, 6292-8.
Lead workers' children are puny, and often die of convulsions, *Abraham*, 6943-9.
Has not observed that children of lead workers suffer unusually, Dr. *Davies*, 8042.
Enamellers' children are emaciated and scrofulous looking, *Ballenden*, 10,512.
An enamel worker had been seven times pregnant; only in one case was the child alive; it only lived a few months, Dr. *Bankier*, 11,695.

GIRLS.

Women, of a younger age especially, more susceptible to lead than men, Dr. *Forbes*, 21.
Anaemic girls should be prohibited from working in lead, *ib.*, 104-9.
Young ones not very much more susceptible to lead than the old ones, Dr. *Debenham*, 465.

I find that the younger ones are certainly more susceptible than the older ones, *Dr. Johnson*, 546.
Young people more susceptible to lead than old people, *Hutchings*, 743.
Younger women more subject to lead than the older ones, *Dr. Baumgartner*, 903.
Many cases of illness from lead in young people, *ib.*, 951-8.
No difference in susceptibility between girls and older women, *Foster*, 1244.
Younger ones decidedly more affected by lead than older ones, *Dr. Whamond*, 1328-9.
Young women decidedly more subject to lead than elderly women, *Dr. Babst*, 1725.
The younger they are the more susceptible to lead, *Dr. Yoakley*, 1826.
Very few employed under 20, *ib.*, 1827.
The younger they are the more susceptible to lead, *Dr. Newton*, 1938.
Young people require the most careful supervision, *ib.*, 2000-1.
The younger they are the more liable to be affected by lead, *Walton*, 2157.
Lose their fresh colour after twelve months' work, *Gray*, 2240.
Some are more susceptible to lead than others, *ib.*, 2240.
Encouraged to seek outdoor employment in the summer, *ib.*, 2241-4.
The younger girls are more susceptible to lead, *Dr. Scott*, 3093.
The stronger and more developed the less danger there is, *Dr. Hay*, 3121-2.
No more susceptible to lead at 18 than at 20, *Dr. Cooper*, 4440, 4468.
Younger women must suffer much more than the older, *Dr. Jackson*, 4776.
Females before maturity are more susceptible to lead than older ones, *Bainbridge*, 5776-8.

APPENDIX 345

Those under 18 or 20 not more susceptible, but less discreet than older persons, *Dr. Parry*, 5898.
After 17 or 18 young women are not more susceptible than older ones, *Vaughan*, 6816-7.
Delicate girls should not be employed if living three or four miles away from the works, *Dr. Bankier*, 11,711-3.
Young girls might show greater predisposition to lead poisoning, *ib.*, 11,734.
Young girls are more susceptible to lead poisoning than full-grown women, *Report*, 13.
No girl under 20 should be employed in a white-lead factory, *ib.*, 18.

HOURS.

10½ hours, exclusive of meals, is a full day, *Walker*, 133
Men at the drying work from 6.0 a.m. to between 12.0 and 1.0, *Cookson*, 762-3.
Women at the stoves work from 7.30 to 1.0, or 1.30; they get away when they have done, *ib.*, 764.
Other women work from 7.0 to 3.30, or 4.0, *ib.*, 794.
Begin at 6 a.m. and get away between 4.0 and 5.0 p.m., *Killoran*, 1104-8.
Start at 6.0 a.m., and are done from 3.0 to 5.0, *Fountain*, 1412-8.
About eight hours daily, *Renwick*, 1477-9.
From 6.30 a.m. to 5.0 p.m., *Mills*, 1524-5.
Works from 6.30 a.m. to 4.0 p.m., *Knight*, 1605-6.
From 6.0 a.m. to between 3.0 and 4.0 p.m., *Walton*, 2143, 2148.
Commence at 6.0 a.m., and finish between 2.0 and 3.0, *Gray*, 2256.
Nine and a half daily at the grinding mills, *Wright*, 2316-20.
Begin at 6.0 a.m., finish about noon, *McVey*, 2383-5.
Average for women, seven hours, *Forster*, 2555, 2561.
Task work should be done away with, *Kelly*, 2651-68, 2678-701.

7.0 to 7.30 to 2.0 o'clock at the stoves, *Webster*, 2963.
Girls work from 7.0 to 1.30; blue stack builders sometimes later, *Kemp*, 3190-4.
Dry stove drawers start at 10.0 and finish at 2.0, *ib.*, 3195.
It is all task work with the women, *ib.*, 3202-5.
Works from 7.0 to about 2.0 or 3.0, *Young*, 3224-6.
Women work from 6.0 to 6.0, *Charlier*, 3282, 3304, 3336-7.
Stoves are drawn in about half a day; from 6.0 to 12.0, *Jefferson*, 3799-800.
10½ hours a day, beginning at 6.0, and leaving at 5.30, *Hultum*, 3962-70.
6.0 to 12.0, at the stoves; never later than 1.0, *Kennedy*, 4588-92.
They generally work five days a week, *ib.*, 4593.
Are too long for such work; every day to 5.0 and 5.30, sometimes to 6.0, *Ford*, 4915-6, 4987-8.
Draws the stove on Saturday, has done at 12.45, *ib.*, 4917-8
From 6.0 to 6.0, *Brook*, 5037-40.
Hours too long considering the nature of the work, *ib.*, 5044-5, 5076-9.
60 hours a week; if hours were shorter and wages better there would be fewer cases of lead poisoning, *Dewhurst*, 5137-41, 5152.
From 8.0 a.m., to 2.0 or 3.0 in the afternoon, *Prisk*, 5188-9.
Usually works 10 hour shifts; doing 12 at present; no general time for starting; comes sometimes at 1.0 o'clock in the morning, *Ashmore*, 5435-40.
Women generally get done at from 3.0 to 4.0 o'clock, *Small*, 5933.
6.0 a.m. to between 2.0 and 4.0, according as they have done their work, but never much after 5.0, *Quirk*, 7241-2.
7.0 to 4.30 in smelting works, *Ashelford*, 8192-3.
7.0 a.m. to 5.0 p.m. in the refinery, *Lewis*, 8235-6.

APPENDIX 347

Spelter men work five hours a day, *Maddox*, 8742.
Enamellers work from 8.0 or 9.0 a.m. to 6.0 p.m., *Orme*, 8908–9.
Feels the hours very long, feels tired from want of food in the morning and the long walk, *Meredith*, 9210–1.
From 8.0 a.m. to 6.0 p.m., and on Fridays, 6.30, *Cooper*, 9693–8.
Does not feel the hours very long, *Bird*, 9899.
About nine hours a day, *Clark*, 9977–80.
From 8.0 a.m. to 6.30 p.m., *Neale*, 11,062.
9.0 to 6.0, *Woodall*, 11,097.
6.0 to 6.0; but the tinners have generally done from 3.0 to 4.0, *Stevens*, 11,353, 11,358.
Works from 6.30 a.m. to about 5.0 p.m., *Homer*, 11,527–8.
From 6.0 in the morning till 5.0 at night, *Stanley*, 12,308.
6.0 a.m. to 5.0 p.m.; a certain quantity of work is given out as a day's work: it can usually be done under the time, *Mackenzie*, 12,418–21.

WAGES.

Women get from 2*s*. 2*d*. to 2*s*. 6*d*., and men 4*s*. 6*d*. per day, *Walker*, 132, 169.
When women used to work at the stoves they had 2*s*. 3*d*. per day; men get 7*s*. 6*d*., *Whiteley*, 266.
Women get 2*s*. 4*d*. a day; men get from 3*s*. 7*d*. to 4*s*. 6*d*., *Hutchings*, 793.
2*s*. a day in the blue beds, *Killoran*, 1102 3.
Women earn half a crown a day at the stoves, 2*s*. in other parts, *Foster*, 1220 6.
12*s*. to 15*s*. a week; it is all piece-work, *Fountain*, 1420.
Red-lead workers get 28*s*. a week, *Renwick*, 1496–9.
About 2*s*. 6*d*. extra for small packages, *ib.*, 1500–3.
2*s*. a day for washing pots, *Mills*, 1523.

2s. a day in the blue beds, *Mack*, 1561.
Earns from £1 a week upwards making wickets; sometimes 4s. 6d. and 5s. a day, *Knight*, 1604–9.
Earns from 11s. to 13s., sometimes more, at smelting, *Long*, 1625-6.
Some of the girls make 18s. a week; smelters get 3s. 6d. a day, *Walton*, 2149-52.
Women get 3s. 6d. to 4s., and men 6s. 1½d. for drawing and setting stoves, *Gray*, 2254–5, 2261.
A guinea a week at the grinding mills, *Wright*, 2314.
15s. to £1 a week smelting, *Ingram*, 2352–5.
2s. to 3s. a day in the blue beds, *McVey*, 2386.
Smelters average 3s. 4½d. a day; blue beds, 3s. 2d.; rollers, 2s. 2¼d.; general work, 2s. 2¼d.; general average, 2s. 4¼d., or adding railway passes, 2s. 6¼d., *Forster*, 2555.
Women 11s. to 17s. a week; men 21s. to 30s., *Kemp*, 3196–200.
Wages 11s. a week at the white hoist, *Young*, 3227.
Women get 9s. a week; the forewoman gets 10s., *Charlier*, 3338.
Foreman has 23s. a week; the girls get 9s., *Curran*, 3544–50.
Girls get 1s. 6d. for putting a stove in, *Jefferson*, 3798, 3849-52.
22s. a week for paint mixers, *Hultum*, 3990.
9s. a week for labelling paint pots, *Oliver*, 4059.
2 guineas a week, and £3 or £4 a year dividend, *Doyle*, 4317-8, 4322–3.
Men in colour works get 4½d. and 5d. an hour, *Peterie*, 4403-4.
Casual workers are half starved; they get 2s. and 3s. a week, *Dr. Cooper*, 4470–1.
Women at the stoves get from 10s. to 12s., *Kennedy*, 4595.
Too little money for the work; from 10s. 4d. to 11s. 8d a week for women, *Ford*, 4915, 4912-5.
Men get twice as much for the same work, *ib.*, 5012.

APPENDIX

25s. a week as foreman in the paint shop, *Brook*, 5043.
Other men get 19s. to 20s. a week, *ib.*, 5081.
19s. a week; a fat lot for 60 hours' work, *Dewhurst*, 5137–9.
Run a guinea a week, *Prisk*, 5219–20.
£1 a week for smelting, *Ashmore*, 5434.
Men paid 18s. a week in the blue beds, 21s. in the stoves, *Chadwick*, 5733.
Men in the white beds get 25s. a week; women in the blue beds, 2s.; for stove setting, 3s. a day, *Small*, 5931–2.
Men get 21s. a week with 2s. bonus, *Tomlinson*, 6110
About a guinea for a full week; cannot stand it to work week by week, *Brown*, 6313–4.
Lead workers are badly paid, *Vaughan*, 6785–92, 6800.
Cannot live well enough on the pay, *ib.*, 6802.
Women get 13s. 6d. a week, *Quirk*, 7244.
Men, 24s.; women, 13s. 6d. a week, *Smith*, 7407–9.
Smelters make generally 5s. a day, *Ashelford*, 8199–200.
5s. 5d. a day in the refinery, *Lewis*, 8240.
Men earn from 3s. 1d. to 4s. a day, *Griffiths*, 8469–74.
Girls earn from 7s. to 14s. a week in the brushing and hollow ware, *Orme*, 9005–6.
12s. a week at the brushing, *Wood*, 9320.
With deductions and alterations of prices, wages of enamellers are below the average for the district, *Hoare*, 9433.
14s. 6d. a week for brushing plates, *Cooper*, 9730.
Earns 12s. to 13s. a week at brushing, *Fellowes*, 9770.
13s. to 14s. a week for sieving, *Bird*, 9900.
Layers-in in enamel works get 32s. a week, *Neale*, 11,048–9.
7s. to 18s. a week for brushers, *Woodall*, 11,093–6.
12s. or 13s. a week for brushers, *Woodward*, 11,186.
Girls are paid by the foreman; he makes a contract with them, *Stevens*, 11,313–6, 11,386–91.

Engages the girls and pays them about 8s. a week, *Robbins*, 11,414–31.
Wipes 20 dozen kettles for a day's work—1s. 4d., *Homer*, 11,531–4; *Scriven*, 11,646–7.
Dippers get 1s. for 20 dozen, *Homer*, 11,535–6.
Wipes 36 dozen covers for 1s. 2d., *Chambers*, 11,575–9.
6s. a week dipping kettles, *Bevan*, 11,666–7.
36s. a week at the Electrical Storage Works, *Stanley*, 12,360.

MISCARRIAGE.

Noticed two cases, *Dr. Johnson*, 560.
One was a washerwoman who was not in the factory at all; the other a cook employed in the outhouse, *ib.*, 561–8, 624.
Attended a few cases, probably due to lead working, *Dr. Baumgartner*, 953, 955.
Lead workers are liable to miscarriages, *Dr. Whamond*, 1376.
Had two before working in white-lead, none since, *Knight*, 1597–1600.
Lead workers have a great many abortions, *Dr. Babst*, 1697.
Frequent abortions among lead workers, *Dr. Yoakley*, 1839.
Lead has a tendency to produce abortion or miscarriage, *Dr. Newton*, 1961–2.
Frequent among lead workers, *Abraham*, 6950.
Knew an enameller who had been pregnant seven times, but in only one case was the child born alive, *Dr. Bankier*, 11,695.

WOMEN.

Women are evidently more susceptible to lead than men, *Dr. Forbes*, 23, 26.
Weak-looking women that apply for work always rejected, *Walker*, 116–8, 121.
Dependent for labour mostly on women, *ib.*, 131–3.

APPENDIX

Women are drafted principally from the lowest class, *ib.*, 180-90.
Would not employ women in white-lead, *Whiteley*, 272.
Women are not so careful as men, *Norton*, 384.
More deaths among them than among the men at Newcastle, *ib.*, 386.
Not more susceptible to lead than men, *Dr. Debenham*, 469-71, 3-5.
Are undoubtedly more susceptible to lead than men, *Dr. Johnson*, 559, 587-90, 619.
Women more susceptible to lead than men, *Hutchings*, 743.
Women are far more susceptible to lead than men, *Dr. Baumgartner*, 950.
Mostly from the lowest classes, *Dr. Babst*, 1694.
Women certainly more subject to lead than men, *ib.*, 1726.
They should not be allowed to work in the stoves, *ib.*
Women now working at Tyne Lead works, with a statement of when they first commenced, and also about the length of time they have been off, *Forster*, 2437-45.
Would have difficulty in doing away with female labour, *Webster*, 2979.
Men are just as susceptible to lead as women, *Fergusson*, 2979-80.
Probably more so, *ib.*, 2980-2.
Generally very poor, badly housed, and ill-fed, *Dr. Hay*, 3115.
Lead workers not very temperate as a class, *ib.*, 3166.
Are steady and respectable, but poorly fed, *Charlier*, 3343-50.
Girls are very respectable, *Curran*, 3523-7.
Keep their hands and faces cleaner than men, *MacArthur*, 3674-5.
Are not more susceptible to lead than men, *Dr. Cooper*, 4467.

Never thought of doing away with female labour, *Kennedy*, 4587.
Women break down more than the men, *Dr. Jackson*, 4761-2, 4774.
Against employing women in lead works, *Thompson*, 5636-42, 5655-61.
Nothing against their employment in blue beds, *ib.*, 5656, 5661.
No harm in women working, *Jordan*, 5689-98.
Statistics show that there does not seem to be any special extra liability more than in case of males. *Bainbridge*, 5765-72.
Not more liable to lead poisoning than men, *Dr. Parry*, 5869-70, 5889.
Should not be precluded from working in lead, *ib.*, 5889.
Cannot express a strong opinion as to whether women are more susceptible to lead than men; there are few women at the works, *Dr. Dobie*, 6011.
No advantage in prohibiting female labour in white-lead works, *Vaughan*, 6722.
Are not more susceptible to lead than men, *ib.*, 6735.
Women with large, melting, liquid eyes should not be employed; they have a tendency to go blind through lead, *ib.*, 6736-39.
Very frequently of a loose class, *ib.*, 6765-9, 6770, 6788.
It is the low wages, not the danger, that keeps people off, *ib.*, 6784-92.
Not more susceptible than men, *ib.*, 6795-9.
Employment of women should be forbidden in stoves and white beds, *Laurie*, 6822-6.
Female labour should be prohibited in the white beds, washing, and stoves, *Abraham*, 6913-6, 6920-1, 6934, 6959-61, 6975-6.
Female inspectors should be appointed for works where women are employed otherwise than in the blue beds, *ib.*, 6922-4, 6974-6.

APPENDIX 353

Nearly always live in a poor neighbourhood, but their homes do not always show neglect, *ib.*, 6939-42.

Lead workers not degraded as a class, *ib.*, 7022-6.

Fact of working in lead makes it difficult for women to obtain other employment, *ib.*, 7030-2.

Are more useful than men in the stacks, *Skerten*, 7356-61.

Substitution of men would very materially increase the expense of manufacture, *Smith*, 7405-6.

Men more able to stand the work than women, *ib.*, 7421.

Eight men do as much work as 12 women, *ib.*, 7424-7.

Women are apparently much more susceptible to lead than men, *ib.*, 7431, 7477.

If women prohibited from working, it might be more difficult to deal with foreign competition, *ib.*, 7436-42.

Personally would not object to women being excluded from the stoves, *ib.*, 7486-94.

Used to employ a good many women; found they were occasionally indisposed with lead colic: gave up employing them partly for that reason, *Risley*, 8339-43, 8364.

Women are more susceptible than men, *ib.*, 8344-5.

Would be equal to lowest class of domestic servants, *Orme*, 8954-7.

Enamellers compare favourably with other classes of female workers, *Hoare*, 9434.

Not generally more susceptible to lead than men, *Dr. Totherick*, 11,756.

Women should be excluded from enamel works altogether, or at least until 21, *Homer*, 11,873, 11,886-7.

If women were excluded from the white-lead, the cost of production would be decidedly increased, *Thorp*, 12,221-5.

With reasonable precautions they are in no greater danger than men, *ib.*, 12,238.

Ought to take the baths more frequently than men,

z

being more susceptible to the effect of lead, *Dr. Williams*, page 262.

Women are more susceptible to lead poisoning than men, *Report*, 13.

No woman should be employed in the white beds, rollers, washbecks, stoves, or packing dry white-lead, *ib*, 19.

Wrist-Drop.

Saw a woman with wrist-drop within three weeks of commencing work, *Dr. Forbes*, 2.

Old cases of wrist-drop are mostly amenable to treatment, *ib.*, 80-2.

Old chronic cases are not amenable to treatment; recent cases may be, *Dr. Debenham*, 501-3.

Chronic cases are better at work than left to starve, *ib.*, 502.

People can go on working with mild forms, *Dr. Johnson*, 608-9.

Is local, and common amongst people handling wet lead, *Dr. Baumgartner*, 971.

Is likely to become chronic if work continued, *ib.*, 975-9.

Drop-wrist uncommon among lead workers; it occasionally occurs, *Dr. Whamond*, 1355.

Usual form of lead poisoning at the Potteries, *Dr. Yoakley*, 1904.

Has seen cases of wrist-drop amongst painters, *Dr. Muir*, 3445.

A man got it several years ago through washing in a tub in which white-lead, carbonised, had been made, *Doyle*, 4303-4.

Is susceptible to treatment, *Dr. Cooper*, 4491.

File-cutters commonly have wrist-drop, *Dr. Jackson*, 4834-7, 4846; *Dr. Gale*, 4896.

Takes a long time to recover from wrist-drop, *Dr. Gale*, 4893.

Had a case about seven years ago; he recovered, but is not working now, is too old; had been working 20 or 30 years when it took place, *Prisk*, 5230-7.

APPENDIX 355

Had an extreme case of a man who was in the habit of drinking beer that had been all night in lead pipes, *Dr. Parry*, 5862–4, 5897.
Not necessarily from the hand being in contact with the lead, *Dr. Dobie*, 6063-9.
Becomes chronic; does not yield to treatment, *ib.*, 6352.
It yields to treatment, but slowly, *ib.*, 7909–12.
Attributable to both local absorption and inhalation, *ib.*, 7913–4.
Does not in the least yield to treatment, *Dr. Samuel*, 8537, 8562, 8581–4.
Glass-makers get wrist paralysis through the lead used in the manufacture, *Hoare*, 9485.
Has known cases of wrist-drop at tinning works where they use all lead, *Clark*, 9996–10,001, 10,014.
Had a man who got drop-hands; he was very dirty; would eat his food with his hands covered with paint, *Merels*, 12,273.

P.S.—While passing these proofs for the Press the *Daily Chronicle* for March 24th comes to hand. It contains an account of a fatal case of lead posioning, which I must quote:—

LEAD POISONING.

At Hanley, on Monday, an inquest was held on the body of Albert Timmis, thirteen, son of A. Timmis, potter's placer, 49, Dresden Street. The lad went in November last (just after his thirteenth birthday) to work in the dipping-house at the Eagle Pottery. He was a delicate boy. A week last Saturday, the 13th inst., he was going on to the works, and when near the gates he fell backwards in a convulsive fit. He was taken home, and the lad died on Thursday last.—Dr. Prendergast said he saw the lad first on the 15th inst. He was suffering from lead poisoning. He had a dropped hand, blue gums, and contracted abdomen, all of which were symptoms of lead poisoning. Witness had seen many cases of lead poisoning, but this was the first that he had seen prove directly fatal. He did not think weak boys should be allowed to work in dipping-houses.—The Coroner said that if the law allowed children who had just left school to work in dipping-houses, which were death traps, the sooner the law was altered the better.

The Chain Makers and Nail Makers

THE condition of the chain and nail makers is so well known, and the documents establishing this condition are so authoritative and so numerous, that it seems almost unnecessary to deal with these trades any further. I would accordingly have allowed my chapters on chain and nail makers to stand alone, an exposure of a lamentable state of things, had I not received a letter, printed in this appendix, from a prominent citizen in the Cradley Heath district, which indicates that some substantiation of my statements is required.

Now in glancing over the pages of the "REPORT as to the Condition of NAIL MAKERS and SMALL CHAIN MAKERS in *South Staffordshire* and *East Worcestershire* by the LABOUR CORRESPONDENT of the BOARD OF TRADE," and of the "REPORT of the SELECT COMMITTEE of the HOUSE OF LORDS on the SWEATING SYSTEM," I find not only substantiation but amplification. I append a few extracts from the Blue Book referred to.

130. With regard to the wages and hours which prevail in these trades, the evidence, though somewhat conflicting on points of detail, leads to certain very

APPENDIX 357

definite conclusions. The facts brought out by the witnesses show that a hard week's work, averaging twelve hours a day for five days out of the week, provides no more than a bare subsistence for the men or women engaged in it. The Rev. H. Rylett, a minister in Dudley, acquainted with the district, stated that the women get from 4s. 6d. to 6s. 6d. a week. A man can make about three cwt. of chain in a week, for which he receives 5s. per cwt., so that he would earn about 15s. One of the work-women said that she could usually earn 5s. a week, or something like that, out of which she had to pay 1s. for firing. Another stated that, working from seven in the morning till seven at night, she could make about a cwt. of chain in a week, for which she was paid from 4s. to 6s. 6d., the price varying. "We do not live very well," she said; "our most living is bacon; we get a bit of butter sometimes." A girl of the age of eighteen stated that she worked twelve hours a day, and that her net earnings would be about 7s. 1d. Sometimes she had bacon for her dinner; never fresh meat. She gave the weight of the hammer which she used at from 7 to 8 lbs., but this was subsequently proved to be a mistake. The average weight does not exceed 3 lbs. It may here be mentioned that the price of a dog chain which is made by these women for three-farthings is, in London, from 1s. to 1s. 3d. The value of the materials would be about 2d. A still more extraordinary case is that mentioned by Mr. Juggins, who stated that cart chains, costing, as far as value of labour and material were concerned, 1½d. and 7d. respectively, had sold in Southport for from 4s. 6d. to 5s., in Liverpool for 5s., and in London for 7s. A male chain maker stated that he earned 14s. or 15s. a week, working from seven till seven, except on Mondays, when he finished at six, and on Saturdays at three. A nailmaker said that out of his week's work only about 8s. 6d. remained for himself, after deducting firing and other charges; "and I have worked for that amount of money," he added, "till I did not know where to put myself." The following case appears fairly representative. The husband and wife work together, and there are three children, two at school and none at work. The man does the "heading," the woman the "pointing" of the nails. Their united work brings in from 18s. to £1 a week; out of that about 2s. 3d. for "breeze," about 5s. for carriage, 2s. 6d. for rent of house and shop, schooling of the children, 6d., 6d. to 9d. for deductions on account of under weight, and the man has to devote from a day to half a day to repairing his tools. Eighteen shillings or £1 does not represent their average weekly earnings over a year, as some weeks they do not get any work at all. Their general hours of work were from seven in the morning till nine at night, with half an hour for breakfast, an hour for dinner, and half an hour for tea for the man. The witness herself had no time, "on account of there being no one in the house to do the work besides myself." The hands employed in factories are better paid, the cases which we have cited being taken from the persons who work in their own homes. Mr. George Green, a member of a firm of nail and chain makers, carrying on business near Dudley, stated that the average wages per week, taken from the books of his firm, running over four weeks, were, "for women, 8s. 2d.; young women, 9s. 4d.; youths, 12s. 7d.; less 12½ per cent., which would be about the cost of their breeze and the rent of their workshop." Referring to men's wages, Mr. Green said he paid by the "list," and that they were getting "on an average 26s. 11d. net"; but in 1888 he thought they would only have been earning "about 22s." These were the wages paid for special quality of work and for superior labour. In the case of the men, thirteen in number, employed on the premises, these amounts represented individual earnings, but as outworkers employ help, the 26s. 11d., in the majority of cases, must be considered as representing the wages of

APPENDIX 359

more than one person. With regard to the half-inch, or common chain, the men would only get 24s. 6d. per week. Out of that sum, Mr. Green said, "you will have to deduct 25 per cent.," leaving the net earnings 18s. 4½d. Upon the whole, we see no reason to doubt the accuracy of the representations made to us by the workers themselves.

As to "Oliver":

134. The work of cutting cold iron by means of the "oliver" falls with great severity on the women who are employed at it, and it appears to us that it ought to be discontinued so far as they are concerned. The oliver is a heavy sledge-hammer, worked with a treadle by means of a spring, and when used for cutting cold iron it is totally unsuited for women. Mr. Kerr said: "I have found among women, especially those that have been working at heavy work, that they are very liable to misplacements of the womb, and to rupture; and also among married women I find that they are very liable to miscarriages, as they frequently go on working when they are in the family way." He believed that women ought not to be allowed to use it at all, and we fully agree with him. It is the out-workers who suffer, not the women in the regular factories. In every respect it is the former class which requires protection: but, as the factory inspectors and other witnesses have shown, they are not willing to be interfered with, fearing a diminution of their opportunity or power to earn the miserable livelihood which, at the best, is at their command.

"Oliver"—and an oliver weighing 36 pounds at that—is still in use in Cradley Heath, although this Committee printed the following recommendation in 1890:—

200. Evidence has been brought before us proving

that the use of the "oliver," or heavy sledge-hammer, used for cutting cold iron, is unfit work for women or girls, with the exception of the "light oliver," adapted for making hobnails; and we recommend that women and girls should be prohibited by law from working the "oliver" when the hammer exceeds a certain specified weight.

My readers will remember my conversation with a woman who had miscarried at every confinement.

The oliver is often so heavy and so much beyond the powers of the frail female being who is yoked to it, that but for the assistance of her children, or of a willing friend, she would be unable to work at all. I saw many women, with three or four little brats each "helping mother," by throwing their weight on to the treadle when the hammer had to be brought down.

The Report deals at length with the malpractices of the fogger, who is fatter and more foggerish than ever to-day, and laments the manner in which the Truck Act and the Factory Acts are set at nought and the Factory Inspectors are deceived and evaded, and to its pages the reader who is desirous of more information is referred. I will conclude with a quotation from paragraph 134, which is more pitiful than anything I can remember to have read.

The mortality among children is great; more than half the total deaths. But this must doubtless be ascribed in part to the early marriages and unhealthy parentage. It is "a common thing" for girls and boys to marry at fifteen or sixteen, and then the parents are living all the time close to starvation. The sorrowful state of their lives is sharply depicted in the statement of one of the witnesses just quoted: "She (the mother) does not get proper attention, but very often gets injury for life from the way she lies in; her children are only a nuisance in the house, and if a child dies, it is, 'Thank God it has gone back again'; if the child survives, it is insufficiently fed, and dies, in a vast number of instances, before it reaches one year."

Aye, indeed, well may the mother thank God.

Letter from a Gentleman at Cradley Heath

9th October, 1896.

SIR,—
I have read with much interest your various articles in *Pearson's* on "The White Slaves of England"; and as one who takes some interest in social matters, I have looked forward with expectation to your article on "The Chain-makers of Cradley Heath." It has been my lot for the last six or seven years to live in the immediate vicinity of Cradley Heath. And as a medical man, practising chiefly amongst the working people, I have been brought into intimate daily (and too frequently nightly) contact with the people, and think I can claim to know something of their habits and surroundings. I am somewhat democratic in my opinions, and in trade disputes my bias and sympathies are as a rule entirely with the employees; yet your description of the chain-makers as a downtrodden, half-starved, and slave-driven class, comes as a revelation to me; and as a revelation which my personal knowledge forbids me to accept, and compels me to suspect (whilst admitting your personal conviction and excellent intentions in the matter) that some of your informants have been "having you on."

I know something of Bromsgrove and the nail trade generally, and admit that the nail-makers there and elsewhere are a poverty-stricken lot, for nail-making is a decaying industry; and had it not been for the allotments, which have made them fairly prosperous, the Bromsgrove nail-makers fairly merited the name of slaves. I do, however, maintain that the chain-makers as a rule are a fairly well paid class, and that their lot contrasts favourably with that of many other classes of operatives.

I have read part of your article over to two or three practical chain-makers—men and women—and they have laughed and remarked, "Oh, no doubt there are such as he describes, but they mostly bring it on themselves." They also draw attention to the fact that your lady informants appeared to be chiefly frequenters of the "Manchester," and surmised that no doubt you paid for a quart or two for them, and that they were not very accurate as to the "copy" which they gave in return.

Of course, in every industry and in every community there are many who are poor and badly paid, and a bad workman or workwoman in the chain trade, as in any other, has an inferior remuneration, although an equal appetite, to his or her more skilful companion. The general idea I gather from your article is that you take unusual and exceptional cases of hardship, and give the reader the impression that this is the general condition prevailing. I know too well, that although Cradley Heath contains a great many contented and industrious workers, it also contains a large number of idle and slatternly people—the class of women who spend the week's earnings on Saturday night, who have beefsteak breakfasts on Sunday, and who do not commence work again till Tuesday or Wednesday, and who then make up for lost time by starving all the rest of the week.

To compare the condition of the chain-makers with that of Dorsetshire labourers, or Bermondsey dock hands, would be most unfair to the latter, and I have lived amongst both these classes.

It is well to remember that the total income of a family here is considerably above the average in most parts of the country, where the family is dependent on the father's work, with that of boys old enough to work; here the mother and daughters contribute to the sum total, and their contribution is additional to the father's income, which elsewhere has to suffice for the needs of the family.

I have often known mothers and daughters go into the chain shop only when they wanted a new bonnet, or to save up a little money for a "good time"—that is, an outing on a Bank Holiday. You would be surprised to know how many chain-makers are the owners of their own houses; how many of them are able to go to Blackpool for a week in the summer; how many of them have good round sums (hundreds of pounds) in the bank. Whilst others, who have had equal opportunities perhaps, exhibit all the signs of destitution, except in their weekly beer account. Go to Cradley Heath on a Bank Holiday, or at the Annual Wake, and the evidences of poverty will be in abeyance. Few there are who cannot afford an outing, and few who do not take a *week's* holiday whenever a Bank Holiday comes round.

There would seem to be two classes in the district: one which exhibits a thrift comparable to that of the French peasantry; and another, with the same opportunities, who live from hand to mouth.

More here than elsewhere, I think it is impossible to estimate a man's financial position from his surroundings. I have known a man with hundreds whose appearance suggested destitution. I have known people with thousands who lived simply in a four-roomed cottage, and did not aspire beyond the social position of their fathers. So much for generalities. Now a few remarks on particular statements in the Article:—

Re *Beer*. "Threepenny" is quite unknown. "Fourpenny" is the usual beer drunk. A great number of the people brew their own beer (their rental allowing them to do so without licence).

APPENDIX 365

Re *Big Chain-makers' Wages.* A cable chain-maker can get £1 a day, of which 12s. goes to himself and 8s. to his striker. Plenty of men do such work four or five days a week. Many after a day or two's work won't work any more that week, but drink for the rest of the week.

Re *Unhealthiness of Work.* "Few old men in Cradley." "Lung Diseases carry men off at early age."

This is most surely incorrect. Consumption is most notoriously rare in this district. All local medical men are agreed that few places in England enjoy such an exemption from Phthisis. Bronchitis and Pneumonia are not more common than elsewhere. Apart from the high infant mortality, which it shares with all industrial centres, and the prevalence of Zymotic Disease, the district and people are very healthy, and the death rate by no means high.

Lucina not a kindly Goddess. Quite true. Confinements as a rule difficult. I have attended many hundreds in this district, *but* none of my worst cases were amongst chain-makers. They are strong, muscular women, and generally have good times, as exemplified by rapid birth of "Little Johnny." Early marriages probably account for Lucina's unfriendliness.

Females swinging heavy hammers. Women are only allowed to make small chain, for which heavy hammers are unsuitable.

3d. a day for blowing bellows. 3s. 6d. is the recognised wage a boy or girl has weekly for blowing. Stringent government regulations prevent children working long hours. Chain-makers tell me that they never heard of a blower working for 3d. a day. So the case must be quite an exceptional one, and yet it is quoted as a usual thing.

Sorrow and hunger, grime, rags, foul food, etc., etc. The chain-makers as a rule, barring exceptional cases, are a *well-fed* (when not at work, *e.g.* Sundays), well-clothed, and certainly a happy people.

Re *Illustrations.*—The third illustration, supposed to represent a female spike-maker, unfortunately does not really do so. The woman is obviously making "hammerchain."

The fifth illustration represents a girl "blowing," with bare feet. I have been in hundreds of chain-shops, but never saw any one working with bare feet.

The year before last was a period of *exceptional* distress in Cradley Heath, owing to the closure of the New British Iron Company's Works; but that is now recovered from, and Cradley Heath seems to be entering upon a period of prosperity.

Whether women should do such work at all is a perfectly legitimate question for debate. For my own part, when I came to the district I had a strong prejudice again women blacksmiths, but further acquaintance with the subject makes me think they might do worse. For young *unmarried* women the work is not unsuitable under present conditions as to hours and class of work. It is *certainly* healthy work. Much more so than dress-making, tailoring, book-binding, etc. Anæmia and chlorosis is not very common amongst chain-makers. The work does not unsex the women. As a class they are much superior to factory girls generally, and especially to "brick-kiln wenches," and such like.

What it seems to me is required is greater combination amongst the operatives themselves. When a strike for a higher list price takes place, there are always so many blacklegs who work at the lower price. All are agreed that the conditions under which women and children work are much better than formerly, but to improve their position there must be a stronger trades combination than prevails at present.

Finally, in my opinion much of the poverty and distress that prevails is due (after drink) to the unjust and iniquitous manner in which the poor law and especially *out-door relief* is administered to aged people, and not to any peculiar slave-driving in the chain trade.

APPENDIX 367

Most pitiable of all is the break up of Friendly Societies when the members get old, and thus provision for old age is lost.

This, however, will not prevail so much in the future, for Foresters Courts are now so constituted that one supports another.

I have met, of course, with many cases of poverty and distress, sometimes from want of work, sometimes from inability to work, frequently from bad administration of a bad system of Poor Law Relief; but such poverty is incidental to all working communities, and in no way peculiar to the chain-trade.

In writing thus, I feel that I lay myself open to the charge of intrusion, and my gratuitous criticisms may find a fitting resting-place behind the fire; but nevertheless, no cause can benefit by the most unintentional exaggeration, and to describe the experience of women workers here as one of "chronic hunger" can only provoke an incredulous smile even amongst the chain-makers themselves.

Day and night for some years I have spent my life amongst chain-makers, and am bound to affirm that although there are exceptionable cases of distress and hardship, such are rather the exception than the rule.

Trusting that you, as a well-wisher to the " horny handed," will receive these remarks from a fellow well-wisher in the spirit in which they are written.

I beg to remain,
Yours faithfully,
X. Y.

Letter from an Oxford Undergraduate

27th *November*, 1896.

Dear Sir,—

As an undergraduate of this university, and one who takes the strongest interest in Social Reform, I venture to write to you respecting the articles which have appeared under your signature in *Pearson's Magazine*. The state of affairs which you disclose are almost past one's imagination, and I hope you will pardon me if I ask you to give me some personal assurance of the terrible facts set down. I take an active part in our Debating Society here, and in fact never lose an opportunity, either in debate, public meeting or private conversation, of trying to arouse interest in the Social Problems of the day. I make this my excuse for this somewhat strange request, for I do not like to adduce arguments, the absolute truth of which I am uncertain.

I should also feel grateful if you would tell me, if, as far as you know, the Church fulfils her mission of succouring the oppressed and boldly rebuking the oppressor, in the districts about which you write. I must not conclude without an apology for encroaching upon your valuable time. I can only plead my earnest desire to become more than a vague sympathiser.

Yours sincerely,

M. N.

R. H. Sherard, Esq.

Conclusion

THE Select Committee of the House of Lords on the Sweating System brought its Report to a close with the following paragraph.

204. We cannot conclude without expressing our earnest hope that the exposure of the evils which have been brought to our notice will induce capitalists to pay closer attention to the conditions under which the labour which supplies them with goods is conducted. When legislation has reached the limit up to which it is effective, the real amelioration of conditions must be due to increased sense of responsibility in the employer and improved habits in the employed. We have reason to think that the present inquiry itself has not been without moral effect. And we believe that public attention and public judgment can effectually check operations in which little regard is shown to the welfare of workpeople, and to the quality of production, and can also strongly second the zealous and judicious efforts now being made to encourage thrift, promote temperance, improve dwellings, and raise the tone of living.

These noble words were written on April 28th, 1890. We are now in March, 1897, and matters are to-day even worse than they were seven years ago. Such, at least, is the opinion I have formed by my investigations. And seven years hence, matters will be still worse unless other remedies are found, than appeals to the stony heart of Capital.

It is a pity that this should be so.

END OF APPENDIX.

Mr JAMES BOWDEN'S Announcements.

NEW NOVEL BY JOSEPH HOCKING.

Crown 8vo, cloth gilt, 3s. 6d.

The Birthright

By Joseph Hocking,

Author of "All Men are Liars," "Fields of Fair Renown,"
"The Story of Andrew Fairfax," &c.

With Three Full-Page Illustrations by Harold Piffard

Interesting as all Mr Hocking's previous novels have been, this is far and away the most interesting he has ever done. It has all his old purity of tone, strenuous moral purpose and manly earnestness, but nothing he has produced before works the reader's interest up to such a pitch of intense, almost painful, excitement. It is in every way Mr Hocking's strongest and most finished piece of work, and justifies the judgment of the reviewer in the *Spectator*, who compared him to Mr Baring Gould, and of other critics who have compared him to Mr Hall Caine, Mr Robert Buchanan, and Mr Thomas Hardy.

AN ANONYMOUS WORK BY A DISTINGUISHED NOVELIST.

Fcap. 4to, cloth.

The House of Dreams

"The House of Dreams" is the work of a novelist who has elected that it shall appear anonymously, though the novels bearing his name have achieved brilliant successes and have won the enthusiastic praise of foremost critics and literary journals. In conception and in boldness of imagination "The House of Dreams" is simply unique, and is likely to make something like a sensation in religious and literary circles. Nothing like it has appeared since Swedenborg first startled the world with his vision of Heaven and Hell, but apart from the daring of the conception, the dream is worked out with such literary distinction, and in such exquisite language, that it cannot fail to arouse intense interest and curiosity.

London: 10 *Henrietta Street, Covent Garden, W.C.*

Mr JAMES BOWDEN'S Announcements.

NEW WORK BY THE REV. FREDERICK LANGBRIDGE.

Crown 8vo, cloth gilt, 3s. 6d.

The Dreams of Dania

By Frederick Langbridge,
Author of "Sent back by the Angels," &c.

With Four Full-Page Illustrations by J. B. Yeats.

"The Dreams of Dania" is a story of Irish life, which is told with such freshness of phrase and imagery, and such rollicking humour that it cannot fail to delight the reader. It ran first in the pages of the *Leisure Hour*, and there it attracted very unusual attention, the *Spectator* singling it out for warm and special commendation. It is by far the finest piece of work that Mr Langbridge has done, and will immensely enhance his reputation.

POWERFUL STORIES OF LOWER LONDON.

Crown 8vo, cloth gilt.

East End Idylls

By A. St John Adcock,
Author of "Beyond Atonement."

Here in these pages are the pitiful tragedies of poverty—the squalor, the vice, and the degradations depicted with the relentless hand of the realist. But though Mr St John Adcock has faithfully painted a picture of "Mean Streets," yet there is not one story—no matter how squalid the subject—in which there is not shown the soul of goodness in things evil.

Truer pictures of slum life have never been drawn, but the artist's touch is always kindly, tender and human.

London : 10 *Henrietta Street, Covent Garden*, W.C.

Mr JAMES BOWDEN'S Announcements

SECOND EDITION. *Long 8vo, cloth, 1s.*

Manners for Men
By Madge of "Truth"
(Mrs Humphry.)

No more comprehensive, up-to-date, and absolutely reliable guide to etiquette has been written than this most useful volume. It is the women-folk of a household—never the men—who are most critical about the manners of guests, and it is by a woman only that "Manners for Men" can be properly treated. The position of the guest whose manners have won the approval of his hostess is already assured, and to read this little volume carefully is the best of social educations for any young man who wishes to acquit himself like a gentleman in Society.

Crown 8vo, cloth.

The White Slaves of England
By Robert H. Sherard.

With about 40 Illustrations by Harold Piffard.

The Contents include:—*The Chemical Workers*—*The Nail-Makers*—*The Slipper-Makers and Tailors*—*The Wool-Combers*—*The White Lead Workers*—*The Chain Makers*—*Appendix.*

This is a terrible and appalling indictment of man's injustice and indifference to man. It is impossible to read the various articles without burning indignation against the slave-drivers and overwhelming pity for the "white slaves." Were it not that Mr Sherard has fully substantiated his facts, one would be inclined to say "such things cannot be." In thus bringing the truth home to the doors of the public, Mr Sherard has done real service to the cause of humanity.

London: 10 *Henrietta Street, Covent Garden,* W.C.

Mr JAMES BOWDEN'S Announcements.

THE FIFTIETH THOUSAND NOW READY.
Long 8vo, sewed, 1s.; cloth extra, gilt, gilt top, 2s.

The Child, the Wise Man, and the Devil

By Coulson Kernahan
Author of "God and the Ant."

SOME OPINIONS OF THE PRESS.

The Bookman says—
"It is the author's special gift to stimulate the minds of Christian teachers. . . . In this little work he has given us work which deserves to live. . . . No one can read these pages without emotion."

The Daily Mail says—
"The writer's views are expressed with bold and manly sincerity, and in a spirit of true reverence. His little book must make a very deep and abiding impression upon the hearts and minds of all who read it to the end."

The Echo says—
"There will be few readers of this work who will not allow with enthusiasm the moral earnestness, the poetic imagination, and the literary charm of Mr Kernahan's stern muse."

The British Weekly says—
"By far the best piece of work that Mr Kernahan has done. . . . The spirit of the age, with its yearnings, its sorrows, its vague aspiration, finds expression in these pages."

The Queen says—
"A work of genius. No one who has read it will ever be likely to forget it."

The Saturday Review says—
"There is a touch of genius, perhaps even more than a touch, about this brilliant and original booklet."

The Illustrated London News says—
"All must recognise the boundless charity, the literary power, and the intense sincerity of one of the most interesting works of the year."

London: 10 *Henrietta Street*, Covent Garden, *W.C.*

Mr JAMES BOWDEN'S Announcements.

Mr WEDMORE'S NEW BOOK.

Crown 8vo, Art Linen, 3s. 6d.

Orgeas and Miradou

With other Pieces

By Frederick Wedmore,

Author of "Renunciations," "English Episodes," &c.

OPINIONS OF THE PRESS.

The Athenæum says—

"The beautiful story of 'Orgeas and Miradou' is specially typical of Mr Wedmore's power of expressing and translating the poignancy of human emotion. . . . It is charged with depths of feeling, and vivid in its extreme reticence and discrimination of touch. In it there is nothing short of divination."

The Illustrated London News says—

"At once pure and elevated in tone and faultless in style. The volume deserves the warmest of welcomes. . . All credit is the author's due for the art with which into this 'dream of Provence' he has imported just the right dreamy atmosphere. . . . It is perhaps the author's masterpiece."

The Globe says—

"It is with episodes only that Mr Wedmore deals, but he crowds into them the suggestiveness of life-times."

The Bookman says—

"The first story is the author's masterpiece; and is among the strangely few perfect short stories in the language. One knows of nothing resembling it."

The St James's Gazette says—

"'Orgeas and Miradou' deals with the most poignant situation that can be imagined. It is the most perfect piece of work Mr Wedmore has given us."

London: 10 *Henrietta Street, Covent Garden, W.C.*

Mr JAMES BOWDEN'S Announcements.

"We put first of the books for girls 'When Hearts are Young' by Deas Cromarty."—*The Christian World* on "The Season's Gift Books."

Crown 8vo, cloth extra, gilt, 2s. 6d.

When Hearts are Young
By Deas Cromarty

With Eight Illustrations by Will Morgan.

OPINIONS OF THE PRESS.

The Manchester Guardian says—

"It is delightful to read. One has come across few recent books that leave a pleasanter impression on the reader's memory."

The Star says—

"There is true insight into the peasant character of the lower fringe of the Highlands. . . . The girl Maggie is true to the life. . . . One is grateful for the *wholesomeness of this gentle story.*"

Lloyd's News says—

"This is one of the pleasantest volumes we have picked up for a long time. . . . It is a tender, beautiful love story, very fresh and wholesome, with a wealth of fine descriptive writing."

The Methodist Times says—

"Deas Cromarty . . . comes in a good second to these great writers (Barrie and Maclaren). *There is the freshness of the mountain breezes about the book which gives zest to the reading of it.*"

The Manchester Courier says—

"*Those who pick up the book will find difficulty in laying it down before the last page is reached.*"

The Methodist Recorder says—

"One of the most charming stories of the season. . . . This is as truly an 'Idyll' as anything Tennyson ever wrote."

London: 10 Henrietta Street, Covent Garden, W.C.

www.ingramcontent.com/pod-product-compliance
Lightning Source LLC
Chambersburg PA
CBHW020307240426
43673CB00039B/733